BIRMINGi

By

Carol Arnall

Published by Carol Arnall 2011

This book is in no way an historic work the stories are simply a miscellany of my own personal memories. If I have made any mistakes I apologise in advance but everything I have written is as I recall it.

Copyright © Carol Arnall 2011

All rights reserved.

No part of this material may be used or stored in any retrieval system without first securing permission from the publishers.

ACKNOWLEDGEMENTS

Thanks to the people listed below who have helped me along the way.

My sister Pauline, always at my elbow telling me to get on with it.

My mom-in-law for her encouragement.

Johnny Godwin, sadly no longer with us but what a brilliant friend and advisor he was. I miss his nuggets of history.

Cousin Maureen for lots of inspiration, encouragement, memories, and a good friend; you are so right, Maureen, Ron and Pauline helped arrange our getting together I'm convinced.

My two cousins Maureen and Shirley, for your tremendous research.

As ever, John, my husband.

INTRODUCTION

My sister Pauline always encouraged me to write the family history.

Unfortunately following a road accident in 1987 I lost many of my early memories. Pauline always promised she would write her memories down but tragically she died before she got round to it. I decided to write as much as I could remember as a tribute to her.

This book is simply a miscellany of my own memories; it tells the story of our early lives in Balsall Heath, Birmingham, where we lived in a back-to-back house with our mom. In no way is it meant to be a historical document. Perhaps, who knows the book would have been completely different if so many of my memories had not vanished following the car accident. If I have made any mistakes with my facts I apologise.

Our father deserted Mom before I was born. She had a desperate struggle bringing us up during and after the war until she remarried. We then moved to Northfield, and we both passed the eleven plus examination to grammar schools. Pauline went to Kings Norton Grammar School, and I, to my dismay, was sent to Bartley Green Grammar School. I was happy at my junior school and certainly didn't want to go to Bartley Green.

I was more than happy when I left the school, and after a few jobs I settled down happily to work at 'Ten Acres & Stirchley Cooperative Society, Birmingham,' as a secretary. Pauline also worked at TASCOS as a secretary to the assistant director, and we were both to meet our future husbands there.

A few years after we married we left Birmingham to start new lives in Staffordshire. I moved to Rugeley, and Pauline to Tamworth.

Despite our lives taking different paths, we always remained close.

The Early Years

Our wedding 21ˢᵗ March 1964

In November 1992, my mother rang and asked me if I would trace the family history, I agreed. At that time, I only had a very vague idea how to set about tracing our ancestors. I thought that you paid a visit to St. Catherine's House in London; looked through some files and that would be that. How wrong I was proved to be.

Mom had mentioned that one of my cousins had the necessary documents that I would need to get me started. I wrote to her asking for copies of anything she might have that she thought would help me. Not hearing anything in the following weeks, I forgot all about it until April 1993 when my mother rang and asked me what progress I was making. I felt ashamed and promptly rang my cousin, who lives in Kings Heath, Birmingham, and asked her if she would help me. On ascertaining that all the old documents were in her loft, I told her that I would telephone again in a few days to see how she was getting on. Realising that I needed to know how to do the research, I bought a booklet on the subject. This proved to be a mine of information and I discovered that various libraries now hold the St. Catherine's House records on microfiche.

One Saturday in May, armed with the information, a notepad, and pen, my husband John and myself decided to visit Central Library in Birmingham. Ascertaining at the information desk that the Genealogy department was on the sixth floor, we made our way via the escalators much to John's disgust, as he prefers the lift.

We found the assistants extremely helpful and were soon set up with the correct census file. I was surprised that so many people resided in one house at that time, and was also intrigued to see the various descriptions of the professions held by members of the family. On that occasion we didn't have any luck with the search, but I consoled myself with the thought that at least I now knew how to set about it, and resolved to return at the first opportunity.

Over the next few weeks, I visited the library a number of times and met a lot of people engaged on similar searches; all as enthralled by the past as I was. I quickly realised I was hooked. The more I found out, the more I wanted to know. Not only did I want to trace my family, I also wanted to know the type of clothes they wore, what their houses looked like, and anything else I could discover. This led to me buying a number of books in the course of my research and spending a lot of time in the reference section of Central Library.

The next step was to find out if anyone in the family had photographs of older family members; my father mentioned that one of his brothers, my Uncle Leonard, had a fantastic collection. I hadn't seen Leonard for many years and at that time he wasn't on the telephone, so I took the bull by the horns and wrote asking if I could borrow a few of his old photographs. To my delight, he wrote back saying that he was planning a book himself, but he was quite prepared to loan me some of his collection. I wrote back immediately asking if we could perhaps meet some time. Apparently, he too had been tracing the family tree on his side of the family.

I mentioned to a friend that I had reached a standstill in my research. She told me that Teletext ran a free family tree service. I sent a letter requesting information on the Clews family, hoping that somebody somewhere could help once it appeared on screen. Whilst waiting, I sent letters out to various family history societies and visited Birmingham Central Library again. My mother and father became even more interested and this led us to swapping stories of times gone by. This only fed what was fast becoming an obsession, and I hoped someone would contact me with information. I decided at that time to write down all that I found out for future generations.

Hopefully, it would also be of some interest to other family members not involved in the research. I waited anxiously for my plea to appear on Teletext.

One evening I was chatting to John about the family history when the telephone rang, and on answering it I was astonished to find it was one of our relatives, whom I didn't know. She had seen my request on Teletext and seemingly she, Shirley, and her sister, Maureen, had done a lot of research back in the 1980s and had unearthed many facts. Shirley kindly offered to send it on to me. We exchanged addresses and agreed to keep in touch. Five minutes later the telephone rang again; it was Maureen and she proceeded to tell me where our ancestors had lived in the 19th Century. I was amazed to hear that they had lived in Romsley, not far from Northfield where I had lived as a girl. It turned out that our forebears had been farmers, nail-workers, and bakers, to name but a few of their professions. Maureen also agreed to keep in touch and send me documents. They had also experienced the same difficulties as I was having - in that we could not trace our great-grandmother's birth certificate and also what had happened to great-grandfather. I promised to pass on the information that I had found.

To say I was delighted to speak to my long-lost cousins is an understatement, and I looked forward to receiving the letter and documents.

When it arrived, I spent a lot of time reading about our relatives of long ago. I realise how lucky I am that Maureen and Shirley kindly passed all the information on to me. It would have taken me years to research and I doubt I would ever have found out as much as they had.

John and I decided to visit Dayhouse Bank, near Romsley where my great-great-grandfather Joseph Clews had lived with his family. Joseph was a farmer and nail-maker. My great-grandmother Sarah Clews had stayed with the family on the Bank for quite a few years. I was hoping to get some photographs, but the weather turned inclement, as it did when we tried again and again...

I took some time out and did some research on where our ancestors had lived and discovered that the land for the small Methodist Chapel at Dayhouse Bank (home of the Clews family) was purchased in 1811. There does not seem to be a record of when it was built, but there are deeds dated 1840 that show it existed at that time. In 1871, it was rebuilt. The chapel was closed in 1965; pity that because I would have loved to have seen the building.

It is said that John Wesley, the famous Methodist minister, stabled his horse at Dayhouse Bank for the night in 1780. It is also said that the Chapel was built over the stable.

In 1823, the first turnpike roads were made; prior to this the roads were nothing but dirt tracks and the villagers of Romsley were cut off in bad weather when the tracks became quagmires.

A Neolithic flint axe head was found on Dayhouse Bank in 1900 when excavation work for a cottage was being carried out. The finder was W. Hill. His son, Captain G. Hill Acc. No.32.36, donated it to Birmingham Museum and Art Gallery.

Despite the busy road at the bottom of Dayhouse Bank, Romsley is still a beautiful area. It was nice to picture young Sarah playing in the fields and lanes around the Bank when she stayed with her grandparents. No doubt, they all went to visit Owen Clews (Sarah's uncle) and his family when he hosted the Manchester Inn at the bottom of the Bank. I visualised the Inn as being a nice cosy little place in Sarah's time, and I was really surprised to discover from the Romsley History Society that I was wrong. Apparently, it was a dank dingy place and a lot of unsavoury characters hung out there. On reflection, I wouldn't imagine Sarah would have spent much time there.

In Sarah's time, the population of Romsley was very small. In 1851, it was 398. Sarah was born in 1856. By 1861, the population had dropped to 377. Unfortunately, the only record of where she stayed up until the time of her marriage in 1875 was found by Maureen in the 1861 census; young Sarah was staying at Dayhouse Bank at the time she was four years old.

Apparently Sarah eloped with a man called Thomas Giblen and married him at Bristol Registry Office in 1875, from that time they never settled anywhere for long.

Sarah's life was a riches to rags story. Her father Charles was a baker and also a farmer so they would have lived quite comfortably. His bakery premises were in Kings Norton. Of course, standards then were quite different to today, and no doubt environmental health would have had a field day then.

Charles married Harriet Dale on March 31st 1856 at St. Martin's Church in Birmingham; her father James was a baker and we think this is how Charles became involved in the baking trade. Joseph Clews, his father, also owned land and he was a nail-master. Joseph left quite a substantial sum of money (for that period) to his sons. His only daughter died quite young.

Returning to Charles' bakery; should he have delivered his bread, it would have been by horse and wagon. The bread dough was more than likely mixed by hand. The first hand-powered mixers were used in Glasgow in 1850. In 1858, Mr Deacon of London was the first baker to use a hand-driven mixer imported from France. In 1858, Ebenezer Stevens patented the first British dough mixer and installed it in his bakery in Islington. It was driven via a belt and pulleys by a steam engine outside the bakery. I don't think Charles' shop and bake house were anything quite so grand.

From census reports it seems Thomas held many jobs of a menial nature, from deal-runner (a person who worked with wood probably to do with the boat building at Bristol) to a street hawker. He was 39 years of age when he married Sarah, and she was 19). Thomas was a widower. On one census return, he put that he was born in the USA. Despite many searches, we have been unable to trace any record of this.

Thomas obviously had a great deal of charm, as he left Sarah many times, but she always took him back. On my grandmother's birth certificate, Thomas put his profession as cook on board a ship. After that, we lose trace of him altogether. He seems to have sailed away into the sunset never to be seen or heard of again. By all accounts, he was a bit of a rogue.

We have searched numerous records without success.

Sarah remarried in 1902, but it seems as if this marriage wasn't happy, as after a few years she reverted to her first marriage name and would never speak of her second husband; the subject was taboo. My Grandmother Lily was born on the 13th April 1893 at Lord Street, Birmingham. Grandmother was registered at birth as a Giblen, but when she married, she took her stepfather's name, Harborne. He was a brass stamper. He married Sarah on Monday 9th December 1902. It was a freezing cold day, the temperature a mere 21° Fahrenheit. There was ice-skating on the ponds and lakes in Cannon Hill Park, Birmingham. Fourteen people fell through the ice despite frequent warnings. Fortunately, they were all rescued.

The law was very hard on offenders in those days; one man, a journalist, was sentenced to nine months hard labour for stealing a post office savings book.

The more I researched, the more my appetite was whetted to find out what I could about the Clews family. I was aware of how hard the social conditions were in those days, and could only imagine the poverty the poor souls had to endure to scrape a living.

Many of the Clews family were nail-makers and it was customary in those days to work from home in a small outhouse attached to the cottage. The whole family were engaged in the work. As soon as the youngsters were able to stand for any length of time, they were taken on to help. They worked long hours for very poor remuneration. The cottages were normally one-up and one-down and as the families in those days were very large, it doesn't take much imagination to picture the appalling living conditions, as the poor people worked hard to make ends meet.

Recording the Family History

Me at Romsley early 1960s

Researching the family history led me to start making notes about my own past and family stories that were passed onto me.

My Uncle Sid, who lived in America, remembers Sarah when she lived in Hope Street, Balsall Heath, Birmingham. Sarah used to sell second-hand clothes in the Rag Market to help scratch a living. This was probably when Thomas Giblen kept abandoning her. Poor Sarah, she certainly had a hard life. She had seven children (four boys and three girls); Grandmother Lily was the youngest. Sarah was obviously a very strong woman emotionally; this has been passed down the female side of the family to Lily my grandmother, to my mother, and her sisters. These women had to be strong throughout the war years, and the hard times that followed. Always wondering when and where the next penny was coming from to help buy food for their families. Unless you lived through those times, it is very hard to envisage the conditions people had to endure. Sid remembers going hop picking in the Romsley area when they were youngsters. They would stay about a week sleeping in a big barn; he wonders if it was one of the farms belonging to the Clews.

My Grandmother Lillian Davies, lived a few houses away from Sarah in Hope Street, Balsall Heath. Sid recalls they slept in the attic; three boys in one bed and three girls in the other, all six in one room. The toilets were down the yard five houses away; there were five shared by twelve families. Six houses one side, and six facing, these were the old back-to-back terrace houses. There was no running water; when needed water was carried from the tap halfway down the terrace, no electricity, only an overhead gas mantle. Two families would do their washing each day in the wash house at the end of the terrace.

Sid remembers walking round Kings Norton with his oldest brother George some years ago. By the roundabout that is at the top of the hill is Cotteridge. The boys wandered across a field then followed a small stream: it might have been the Rea. George said this was where some of Lily's relatives used to live. Unfortunately, this was before Sid became interested in the family history or he would have followed the trail. George pointed out a small church near the roundabout that his mother used to go to when she was a child.

My mother recalls that a Mr Moore was the headmaster when she attended Hope Street School. There was also a Miss Rachael, who shared her sandwiches with my mom. There was a Miss Taylor, who, insisted Mom should have the chair she had used in the staff room when she retired from the school. It was a collapsible wooden chair with tapestry worked on the back and seat. Mom kept it until she was eighteen when unfortunately it broke.

My sister Pauline and I lived in Coneybere Street, Balsall Heath, with our mom during the mid to late 1940s - up the terrace as it was called - Newport Terrace to give it its proper name. It was a back-to-back house at the top end of a row of terraced houses. It was a two-up and two-down house with a patch of ground outside the front door, called the garden, but I can't even remember weeds growing in it let alone flowers. The washhouses were at the top of the terrace where the women took it in turns through the week to do their washing. I see the old mangles and boilers fetching a small fortune now at the antique fairs. We never thought where we lived was a slum. Why should we? We knew of no other life except that small house at the end of the row.

We would jump over the side fence to go to the toilets housed in the yard. From what I can remember, there were only about eight toilets for the whole terrace. We shared with neighbours from along the row, early unisex communal toilets.

The only memories of the very early years I have are when Mom sat me on the side by the sink and gave me some cod liver oil followed by a spoonful of malt. I was very young then, no more than two or three I should say. The malt was delicious but the cod liver oil diabolical.

Mom told me she would carry us girls down Coneybere Street first thing in the morning to take us to the nursery in Parker Road, run by Matron Green. She worked in a machine factory. It must have been really hard for her struggling through the war years to bring us up.

I never knew my father as Mom divorced him soon after I was born and he never saw me. I do have lovely memories of my grandparents in Derbyshire. They must have thought a lot of us girls as they kept a photograph of Pauline (my older sister) and me on their sideboard. This is the photograph I used for the book cover.

I remember when we were staying with them once and recollect Mom getting up very early one morning, we shared her bed, and she disturbed me as she was dressing. I called to her as she was creeping out of the bedroom and she whispered, 'Go back to sleep, Carol.' I was frightened thinking that we would never see her again. In fact, I found out later she had gone to Birmingham to find work and a house so we could all live together. Mom seemed to be gone forever and I missed her so much. I would spend hours in the front room with my nose pressed to the windowpane, steaming the glass up with my breath, and then making squiggles down the pane, looking to see if she was coming to fetch us. I do not think she was away that long, it just seems long when you are a child. When she returned, she took us back to Birmingham where she had found a house and a job; my mom was a very independent and strong woman. It would have been all too easy to have us put in a home or have a relative look after us. Not Mom, we were her girls and no one else was going to have us.

Our grandparents lived in an old farmhouse in Market Street, Normanton, Derby. I have never been there since growing up, but Pauline went in the 1970s after tracking our relatives down. This is how I know about the photograph being on the sideboard. At the time of Pauline's visit, our father was out walking and I don't think she ever met him. I had no real interest, as I thought he had been rotten deserting my poor mom and leaving her with two youngsters to bring up and with no income or means to support herself, let alone us. 'Why on Earth,' I asked Pauline, 'would I want to know about him?' I did have a letter from a distant relative in the late 1970s to say he had died. I was surprised how upset I was and sorry that he had died so young; he must have been in his early sixties. Sorrow, in so much that he never made an attempt to see his daughters in the flesh so to speak, and get to know us. To him his legal daughters were frozen in time in the photograph that stood on his mother's sideboard. I say legal because I do know that when he was in Italy during the war he met a woman and had two children by her. So out there, we have half-kith and kin. In this country, there are also other half-brothers and sisters whom we are destined never to meet.

The Very Early Years

When I was born, Mom was so poor she couldn't afford a cot, didn't even have a drawer to put me in. My crib was an orange box. Many people have told me they were poor when they were young, but when I listen to them, I realise that perhaps they weren't rich, but compared to us they were wealthy.

St. Albans Church was just across the road from the terrace where we lived, and we girls would go to the Sunday morning service and also Sunday school in the afternoon. If we missed a service, we would receive a postcard through the letterbox with an arrow pointed at an empty seat. These were delivered by one of the nuns from the church. Mom always said how good the nuns were to her. I don't know in what way, but obviously, they helped her along when she was struggling to bring us up. There were two priests at the church, but the only name I can remember is Father Peel, I don't remember the other priest's name, but they were always kind to us. It was, as far as I know, a High Church of England and I can still remember the smell of the incense when the priest walked down the aisle swinging the mace, it was a very powerful aroma.

I can remember the kids down the terrace yelling at us girls, 'Ya yow aint got a Dad ya ya.' The day that sticks out most in my memory is when Mom called Pauline and me into the house. We were sitting on the doorstep having a chat. Mom told us to call Les, whom she had been going out with, 'Dad' from then on as they were now married. I was down the terrace like a shot, sticking my tongue out at the kids saying, 'Got a Dad now so there.'

'You aint,' they shouted back, but they soon realised we had. What a proud moment that was.

13

Another vivid memory is the day Mom had her teeth out. Pauline and I were sitting on the doorstep; our favourite place to chat. Dad called us indoors and there was poor Mom with a bucket by her with blood oozing from her mouth. We shrieked in shock and then she smiled at us and we screamed loudly as her teeth looked so huge. She had been fitted with her new set of teeth and they were covered in blood. Poor Mom, she must have felt awful at having her teeth out, without us screaming in terror at her as well.

One incident that still makes me shudder when I think about it is one night when Pauline and I were fast asleep in our shared double bed I was disturbed by a rustling coming from the end of our bed. I woke Pauline, saying, 'There's something moving under the blankets, at the bottom of the bed.' We both started screaming and Mom came rushing in and pulled the blankets up from the bottom of the bed. Horrors, the cat had had kittens in the bed. Oh, I've never forgotten that, it's put me off cats for life. The mess and the smell remain a bad memory.

Grandma Davies, Mom's mother, lived in Clevedon Road not far from Calthorpe Park in Balsall Heath, Birmingham. She had nine children and looked after a friend's son, Leslie. Pauline and I would often walk to see her. We would hasten up the long dark entry that ran alongside the house in fear of our young lives, in case a bogeyman jumped out of the dark to get us. What a relief when we opened the gate at the top and were safely inside Gran's house. The gate led us into a small vestibule; one way led into the parlour and kitchen, the other along the hall to Gran's sitting room. There was a heavy curtain hanging behind the sitting room door to keep the warmth in, thick red carpet on the floor, and all Gran's treasures were placed around the room. The majority of the ornaments were what Gran had brought back from India. Just behind her chair, another door led into a walk-in cupboard; this door was also covered by a thick heavy curtain. In here were more of Gran's treasures and we children loved to get in there and have a good old rummage.

It was a large house with quite a number of bedrooms – I don't know how many – I do remember that various aunts and uncles often stayed with Gran and the house never seemed crowded.

The room at the front of the house was often occupied as well; that's what I remember about my Gran's home there was always a friendly family face around. There was a lovely atmosphere that pervaded the whole house. We were always made welcome whenever we visited. It was lovely, as soon as you entered any room it was as if you were being greeted by an old friend.

Granddad worked on the railways. He died while I was quite young so unfortunately I have no memories of him. He was very well liked as whenever the family mentioned him, they spoke fondly of him.

We were never short of aunts, uncles, and cousins with Grandma having such a large family.

Everyone congregated in the parlour when visiting Gran. The kettle was permanently on and there was always a story to be told by one or other of the visiting family, as they sat drinking their tea grouped around the kitchen table.

My Gran was a lovely woman, always smartly dressed, with her blonde hair tightly waved. She always coloured it saying she was blonde when she was born and she would stay blonde until she died. Gran was a real lady.

Despite having a large family, if Mom couldn't use the nursery, Gran would always look after us while Mom was working.

Mom told me that Gran would put her best clothes on and go to the races at Ascot once a year. I would love to see a picture of how she looked in her smart clothes.

Of course, we never thought of ourselves as being poor. It is only when you look back through the years that you realise just what a struggle those times must have been. A few years ago, Pauline rang and said how much Mom must have loved us to work so hard. I agreed thinking how we take so many things for granted now.

One story about Gran is fascinating; when Granddad was in the army in 1923, he was sent with his regiment to the Northern Territories of India. Gran followed with the children by boat, my Mom was only a baby and she was taken very ill on the way to India. Mom was so ill, they thought she had died; they were about to bury her at sea when she uttered a small cry, which obviously saved her young life.

I think my Gran was a very brave lady trekking out to India with eight small children. How they survived is nothing short of miraculous; the heat was terrible, let alone the journey there and back, managing to cook, feeding eight youngsters, and clothing them. Conditions would have been very primitive indeed in those days.

When we were older we used to go to Moseley Swimming Baths and one warm summer's day, Mom sent us off with our costumes and towels. The people were queuing round the block to get in and eventually our turn arrived. We duly paid our fee and hurried to change, looking forward to cooling off. Just as we entered the pool area, a lifeguard approached us and said, 'Okay your time's up.'

'No it's not,' Pauline told him. 'We've only just arrived.'

He wouldn't have it, saying, 'I've been timing you two, now on your way.'

Pauline tried again, saying, 'Look, our bathing costumes aren't even wet.' No good, we were sent on our way. Mom couldn't believe it when we arrived home so early, and now whenever I hear the song, 'My bathing suit never got wet', my thoughts return to that day.

A few years after Mom re-married, I remember Pauline was taken ill with Scarlet Fever and Mom took me on the tram or trolley bus to the isolation hospital to visit her. That was the only time we spent apart until we left school. I also had Scarlet Fever, but that was when we lived in Northfield. I spent a week or so in bed feeling guilty because poor Mom had to bring all my drinks and food upstairs to me whenever I felt like eating. Scarlet Fever was no longer considered such a dangerous disease then, as antibiotics were used in the treatment.

We got our pocket money on a Saturday and we would spend it at the little shop at the end of the terrace. I think the shopkeeper's name was Mrs Perks; she was a nice lady. We would buy sherbet and make pop with it in the summer; sherbet fountains were delicious as were gobstoppers, and I would always have to have a comic, usually, *The School Friend*. It was my favourite comic. Mom read it one day and after that, she called me Dilly Daydream as one of the girls in it was known as that; the girl daydreamed her way through life and wore the same kind of National Health specs as I did. I didn't mind the family calling me that as I did daydream and I lived in a fantasy world, where I was secretly a beautiful princess and one day soon people would realise and then I would be transported off to a beautiful palace somewhere in the world. I'm still a daydreamer but my dreams are a lot more realistic nowadays.

From the library along Moseley Road, I would always borrow Enid Blyton books. They saw me through my childhood years following the adventures of *The Famous Five*.

I can just about remember listening to the radio on Saturday lunchtimes whilst we were eating bubble and squeak, I loved that meal and looked forward to it all week. Then nine times out of ten, Mom would give us the money to go to the pictures.

Pauline and I would go to the sixpenny crush at the Triangle Picture House at the bottom of Coneybere Street on a Saturday afternoon. Our heroes were Roy Rogers and Trigger, his horse. He was a cowboy and what adventures he would have as he galloped across the screen, us kids cheering him on as he chased away the Indians and gangsters. We would cheer and boo with the best of them. There was Tarzan and Jane, and also Bill Boyd, another cowboy who we would sit in awe of. It was exciting stuff to us kids.

I remember one time, Mom was cutting my hair and I moved, her scissors slipped and catastrophe, I landed up with hair shorter than any boy had. Standing in the queue that Saturday, all the kids got onto me saying, 'Look at that funny boy with a dress on.' It was awful but Pauline was there for me, telling them to shut up. If she was around, no one could pick on me without her being first to jump to my defence.

Other times we'd go up town and on the way home, Mom would buy us hot potatoes from the potato man who stood on the corner at the bottom of Coneybere Street. A paper cone of his spuds warmed you up on a cold winter's day. They tasted as good as they smelt. Overall, Saturdays were great.

Mom was a wonderful cook; my father enjoyed tripe and onions but I hated the sight of it, ugh, just seeing it used to make me shudder. We enjoyed rabbit stew as well, but nowadays, of course, I would run a mile sooner than eat rabbit. A few years ago, one of my dogs ran off into some scrubland and when I found her, she was eating a dead rabbit, what a horrible sight that was and did I have a job getting it off her.

Thinking of us all sitting around the table reminds me of our beautiful Sunday afternoons' high tea. Mom would make an enormous salad followed by peaches and cream and one of her delicious sponge cakes. The boys had a habit of plucking the celery sticks out of the jug and flicking the water at us, then they'd collapse laughing with delight at the shock on the receiver's face.

Nobody could beat Mom at cooking, she made the most marvellous dinners, cakes, pancakes, you name it she could turn her hand to it and we took it all for granted, but looking back I realise just how skilled she was to be able to make good wholesome meals on a tight budget in the early days. Then as our circumstances improved, she was able to turn her hand to more fancy cooking without any training whatsoever. I never saw her use a cookbook. Her Christmas cakes were 100% better than any shop-bought cake. She made three-tier sponge cakes filled with butter cream and jam, jars of strawberry jam, and blackberry and apple jam. Mom also preserved jars upon jars of pickle, pickled onions, chutney, and pickled red cabbage.

In the early 1950s, I remember being fascinated when a telephone box appeared at the bottom of Coneybere Street. My Aunty Joyce (Mom's youngest sister) went in and made a phone call. I thought it was wonderful and wanted to call someone up myself. I found it difficult to comprehend how a telephone worked. To me it was quite magical.

We loved going round the Bull Ring Markets. The stallholders were always friendly and would often give us girls an apple or orange each. All of them would remark how beautiful Pauline was. She was, with her blonde wavy hair and beautiful little face. Pauline got her good looks from Mom, who's also beautiful, always has been. Funnily enough, I never minded people remarking on Pauline's good looks, just accepted that she was and felt proud of her.

Hide and Seek was one of our favourite games at that time, also hopscotch, skipping, and tig; there were a few others that I seem to have forgotten. A couple of years ago, my grandchildren wanted to play hopscotch in the street outside their home; as they were busily chalking it up, one of the neighbours came out and shouted at them for messing up the pavement! I remember thinking what kind of society do we live in when youngsters aren't allowed to play innocent games outside.

One of the things I have never forgotten is holding my arms outstretched so Mom could wind her skeins of wool. If there were a lot to do, I would hang the hank of wool over the back of a dining room chair and wind it like that, as it was so much easier on the arms. Fortunately, wool comes ready wound nowadays making life that much easier.

I have a memory of living in a small house in a wood, and of Pauline and me going outside in the very early morning to milk the goats. It was at Leominster and that's all I can remember of what must have been quite an adventure for us two. Mom never told me why we lived at the house in the woods.

In the fifties, we were re-housed to Northfield. As we were leaving Coneybere Street, a sack of coal fell off the lorry. Pauline and I were sitting in the back and shouted to Mom as loud as we could to stop the lorry. Mom replied, 'No, we're going to leave it as it's a sign of good luck.' I remember thinking how strange as in those days, lumps of coal were like pieces of gold. However, left it was, and I could imagine how quickly it was picked up as we drove on.

We moved into 43, Barnsdale Crescent, Northfield. Our family had grown by then so the extra rooms were great after that tiny house in Balsall Heath.

The new house was behind the green, it was third in a row of (I think) five houses. The first thing I noticed was a red telephone box on the green; to me that was magic, a phone box all to myself, I thought in my childish innocence. Telephones fascinated me, I was astonished that by picking up a receiver and putting a few numbers into the telephone, you could actually speak to somebody miles away.

The next astonishing thing I discovered was we had a front and a back garden; in the front garden were orange and red flowers and grass. Many years later, I discovered the flowers were nasturtiums and marigolds. The back garden had a lawn either side of the path running down the centre.

As if all that wasn't enough, the house had a bathroom and an indoor toilet, plus quite a large kitchen and, three bedrooms. At that stage of my life, I did not know houses could be that large. I really thought we had landed in Paradise.

The day we moved in, Pauline and I were looking after the younger ones in the back garden while our parents were unpacking our belongings. The children from 41 called across the fence to us, and on looking round I thought I was seeing double; two young girls were standing looking at us. I blinked a few times trying to work out what was wrong; the girls looked exactly the same as each other to me. I had never seen or heard of twins before and for a few minutes, I was dumbstruck. Pauline was chatting away to them and discovered they were known as the Fulwell twins. We got to know the girls' quite well so I am shocked

21

that I have forgotten their Christian names. I can remember going to one of their birthday parties and thoroughly enjoying it. They were identical twins and it took me many years to tell them apart.

We soon made friends with other children, and off we would go to play down Merritt's Brook. At first, I couldn't believe that we could actually play in these wide-open spaces called fields. A crowd of us went down the brook one day and one of the gang had tied some rope around a tree branch so we could swing like Tarzan (another one of my heroes) across the brook, all good fun. One day, I decided I was going to climb a tree, but unfortunately, I got stuck quite high up and had a panic attack, preventing me from climbing down again. I don't know where the man who got me down came from, but was I glad to be back on firm ground. I never tried it again.

I remember dragonflies hovering over the water, I was terrified of them as the kids told me they gave you a terrible sting and you could die from it. I was afraid of them for many years. Damselflies and mayflies darted to and fro, flashes of blue and silver turning everywhere into a magical playground for us kids. Kingfishers would skim along the brook adding to the enchantment of the day. We would go blackberry picking in the early autumn; more went into our mouths than the basin Mom provided. Strangely enough, we never worried about eating grubs or even washing the berries. They were like shining black glistening jewels hanging, just waiting to be picked and eaten. I certainly would not go, picking, and eating them now without a thorough investigation. Nevertheless, that's one of the joys of childhood: no fears of being ill from eating the summer bounty.

I quickly came to accept this new way of life away from the back streets of Old Birmingham. In a recent letter to my mother-in-law, I mentioned that there are high-rise flats where we used to play, instead of fields with the babbling brook gurgling its way through. Hard to imagine how they could destroy all that beautiful countryside.

I remember the welfare was up St. Heliers Road and we would go and collect the bottles of orange juice and horrid cod liver oil for the latest baby, with our ration books that were then duly stamped.

Our doctors' surgery was on Frankley Beeches Road. If my memory serves me right, it was on the corner of Hogg's Lane. There was a Dr. Morris and a Dr. Davies, and I think the other doctor's name was Watts. Dr. Watts was rather fierce and we dreaded having to see him, whereas Dr. Davies was quite young and very attractive, all the young girls thought he was a real dish and some went to see him on any pretext.

Mom had a need of urgent treatment at the doctors at least twice, one day she cut herself badly when she was opening a tin of corn beef. She hurried off up Hogg's Lane to the docs. I sped out to the phone box on the green to call Dad and he left work early to come home. By then, Mom had returned with a huge bandage on her hand. She was in a lot of pain for a few days. Another painful experience was when she had a whitlow on one of her fingers and I can still remember her wincing with the pain from it.

One bonfire night, Mom was sitting quietly feeding one of my brothers, I think it was Peter, and Dad was working overtime, when all of a sudden the letterbox rattled and there was a huge bang. Someone had shoved a firework through the box. Mom jumped, the baby started to howl, and I lost my temper and told Mom I was going to phone the police. Mom was shocked not only by the firework but also at seeing me getting mad. Normally, I was the quietest and most placid of the family. I ran outside to the phone box on the green and called the station. A policeman came round at once and took the details. Of course, it was too late to do anything to find the people who had done the deed, but at least I felt as if I'd done something.

A Mr and Mrs Stevens and their son lived at number 39. I can remember Mrs Stevens banging on the wall and then the front door of our house; she was very upset and crying as she told us, the King had died.

We attended Trescott Road School. The only memory I have of that school is that Pauline and I went to join the school together without Mom or Dad, I don't know where they were. Mom may well have been having one of the children. They took our details and I remember one of the teachers saying how grown up we were to go on our own. The rest of our time there is a blur.

My cousin Maureen has a very early memory of Trescott School. She remembers being in the nursery and being put in one of the beds for an afternoon sleep, obviously Maureen must have been very young when this happened.

After Trescott Road School, Pauline and I attended Tinkers Farm Junior School. I enjoyed my years there and got on famously with all the children and the staff. I recall there was an open day for the parents and our class were going to recite a poem. I was so proud to be chosen to announce the poem. I begged Mom for a nice dress to wear and she found a brown taffeta one for me. Did I feel grown up or what! I can still feel that lovely material on my legs and hear the swishing sound it made as I walked along. As I stepped out of the line and announced the poem *Sea Fever* by John Masefield, I thought I would burst with happiness. Tinkers Farm School really made me feel accepted and a person in my own right. My lasting memory of the school is of being happy.

Whilst at Tinkers Farm School, I sat the eleven-plus examination. I made no effort whatsoever to pass as I was adamant that I didn't want to change school, but to my great astonishment and disappointment, I passed. Pauline had also passed. She was allocated a place at Kings Norton Girls Grammar School, and I was allocated a place at a newly built girls grammar school in Bartley Green. I didn't want to go to the new school; being happy at Tinkers Farm the thought of leaving all my friends behind upset me deeply, but go I did, I had to. When Mom said you had to do something, you did it with no arguments.

I hated Bartley Green Grammar from day one. With hindsight, it was a forgone conclusion that it was going to be an unhappy experience. I didn't want to go, but I had to; however, no one could make me like the place.

It was quite a long way to travel to school, Mom bought me a second-hand sit up and beg bike that I had to learn to ride; I had to have quite a few practice runs. Never having a good sense of balance, I took quite a few falls before I got the idea of how to stay on. I had no clue where the school was, so before the first term began, I would head off in the general direction of it and pray I would get there. I would find my way to Frankley Reservoir, proceed past then cycle along a narrow leafy lane to Hollywood, turn right at the top of the hill and follow the road for a mile or so to the school. You couldn't really miss the place as it was at the top of a steep hill. I would always push my bike up all the hills, I never had a good pair of lungs, plus my bike had no gears and it was so old anyway sometimes it was quicker to walk. I wonder now how it held itself together.

I was forever having punctures and then on trying to repair it, the tube would blow out with such a loud noise everyone in the vicinity would jump out of their skins.

The school was very hard to get to by public transport. If Dad couldn't drop me off, I had to take the bus from Merritt's Brook Lane, get off at a point along the Bristol Road, and then catch another bus. In addition, it was all extra money out of the housekeeping. After a few dry runs at the journey by bike and by bus, I became pretty confident that I would find the school.

Before starting though, I had to acquire a school uniform. Horrors, the colours were green and yellow. My first thought was I would look like a wasp. The only comfort was so would all the other girls. One of my aunties was a first-class dressmaker and she offered to make as much of the uniform as possible. I thought this was very kind of her, but it meant a very long bike ride from our house to Quinton. Not just once either as the first visit was to be measured, next to be fitted, the final trip was a check to see all was in order, and that was that. All I can remember of the journeys was the heat. It was August, each time the sun seemed to beat down relentlessly, and I would arrive at Aunty Lee's house hotter than I had ever been in my life.

Looking back now, I wonder how I got through the first months at that school. I soon became the butt for all the bullies in the school. Up until going to that school, Pauline had always protected me from any kids who were nasty to me, so here I was in a completely new environment and nobody to hold my hand. I suppose many would call it growing up, but I had no one to guard me from the cruel jibes of my tormentors. Some days were like a living hell and I don't know how I endured them. Most lunch times were spent around the back of the school sitting on the steps, waiting for the bell to ring to call us back to lessons.

The only thing that saved me from being wretched all of the time at Bartley Green School was when I struck up a friendship with a girl from the next crescent (Honiton) to ours, Hazel Stokes. We would ride our bikes to school every day - well most of the time we would push them due to my bike being so old.

It was a lovely journey to and from school along the country lanes. Walking or cycling along the road that ran alongside the reservoir, chattering our heads off, or more often than not laughing so much we nearly wet ourselves. We dawdled our way there and were rarely on time. It was the same coming home, laughing and giggling while pushing our bikes up the hills.

I was not an apt pupil by any means. I certainly didn't excel at any subject. The only lessons I really enjoyed were English Literature and cookery. The English and cookery lessons were taken by Miss Burrows; the lessons were made interesting, and I could lose myself in these subjects. Scripture as it was then called was interesting as was music; the same teacher, Miss Harnott, took both of these. I found researching the great music composers fascinating, and frequently my compositions received a good mark from Miss Harnott.

Because of the bullies I would often take an afternoon off school by saying that I had to attend the Eye Hospital in Birmingham. I would catch the bus into town and walk around the shops looking at all the goods for sale. Then I'd catch the bus home and arrive home around my usual time. Mom would not have been very happy if she knew what I was up to. In fact, she would have been really angry. But to me, Mom's anger was more bearable than the bullies; I think in a way I wanted her to find me out so then I could tell her what was going on. But she never did.

The Asian flu swept through the school; I think it was about 1958. Miss Pickwick, who taught games, took me home in her car; there was another teacher with her, but I cannot remember her name. I don't know if the school closed, but the Asian flu swept across the country and caused many deaths.

We were the first teenagers; a name coined for us when rock and roll began. It was a wonderful era to live through.

This was the time of 45 rmp records extended players; of course there was no such thing as a CD or computers. The popular tune on a record was on the A-side and the not so popular on the back. The thing was sometimes the B-side became more popular than the A-side.

In the music shops were small booths where you could put on a pair of headphones and listen to your favourite record.

When we first had a television, I can remember watching a program called *Lunch Box* hosted by Noele Gordon, we really enjoyed it and Mom always said she would like to meet her. (Noele Gordon eventually was to star in the hit soap *Crossroads* playing the part of the motel's manager.)

As we grew older, so we developed schoolgirl crushes on our film idols. Pauline's biggest idol was the film star James Dean. He wore huge sweaters, we called them Sloppy Joes and they became the in-thing to have. Of course, we had to have one each and felt the bees' knees in these huge woollies. I expect they are what are now known as bum-huggers. He also made smoking a cool thing to do as he was often photographed with a cigarette in hand, standing looking sulkily into space. We didn't follow him with the smoking; that came later with me. Pauline never smoked and neither did Hazel.

Elvis Presley was my idol; with his beautiful singing voice and dark good looks, he was the epitome of youth to me. We enjoyed the newfound maturity in being able to have our say in music, films, and fashion. Looking back, it was a wonderful time to be young. It was the first time youngsters had a say in what they liked and expected from life. The following generations have benefited and if we now think that perhaps they have too much say and freedom, maybe we should stop and realise that we were the ones who started it and time has to move on.

Having made friends with Hazel, we would bop together in the school gym at lunchtime to Elvis records, much to the amazement of the teachers. They stood and looked on awestruck, never having seen anything quite like it in their lives. The Dashing White Sergeant was more in keeping with that era. We were lucky to be in at the beginning of the rock and roll years; it was wonderful music to let your hair down to and jive the hours and frustrations away.

When I first started at the school, I was in form 2B, Miss Burrow's class. She was a nice kind teacher who made her lessons interesting; you felt that you wanted to learn. One day we were to make a steak and kidney pie. Mom bought me the ingredients but unfortunately, I had to take the bus that day and left the bag of goodies on the bus. That was one day I couldn't participate in the lesson, and I got into double trouble from the teacher and Mom for being so careless. I was more than likely daydreaming again about going anywhere apart from school.

Mrs Mackie was the headmistress of the school and she always dressed in black. Frankly, I was terrified of her. Part of the uniform was a green gabardine coat. Well, poor Mom couldn't afford to buy me one along with a few other things. I was frequently called up before the head for not wearing the full regulation uniform. Much as I explained our circumstances, it fell on deaf ears and I was always on report.

I never told Mom of this dilemma as I didn't want to worry her. She had enough on her plate trying to make ends meet feeding and clothing us all. By this time, there were six of us. Our family had certainly grown in the last few years. When Mom had my young sister, I fell in love with her, as did everyone else. She was so sweet; blue eyes, blonde hair, and a sweet nature to go with it. I confess I spoilt her, as did everyone else who met her. Out came my knitting pins and soon I was producing cardigans and jumpers for her. Even as she grew older I carried on knitting turning out amongst other things a lovely peach-coloured dressing gown. She was a beautiful young girl and I hoped that when I married - there was never a doubt in my mind that I would marry - I would have a daughter first and that she would be like Jane. I wanted a son, of course, but a daughter first.

Some of the names from school that I remember are Jean Davies, her married name is Price; Mary Hornsby; and Hazel Stokes, who became my best friend; Jennifer Owen-Smith, and Anita Spriggs.

One occasion that unfortunately I can never forget is when Hazel and I arrived at school early one morning for a change, so we decided to go looking for our friend Anita. We made our way to the classroom where she would normally be, immediately on entering the room we knew something was wrong, it was so quiet, you could feel a terrible sadness hanging in the air. Not seeing Anita, we asked one of the girls where she was, the girl was very upset and told us that Anita was dead. Such shocking news obviously upset us very much, and we later found out that our friend had committed suicide.

Anita was a tall good-looking girl who had recently lost quite a lot of weight and had grown her hair long, I remember envying her good looks. We never discovered why this had happened, and it left its mark on us. It was so hard to take in that your friend could put pillows on the kitchen floor, turn the gas taps on, lie down, and gas herself.

The press got to hear about it and the reporters were waiting at the bottom of the school drive when we finished school. We ignored them, cut them, in fact. As if we could talk about our friend after losing her in such tragic circumstances.

One sunny summer's morning, I was riding along Shenley Fields Road with Hazel, we were on our way to school. I noticed a coal delivery lorry up ahead and for some reason or other, I lost my concentration and fell off my bike, hitting the road with an almighty thud. A policeman appeared from nowhere, took me into someone's house, and bandaged my badly cut knee. Hazel carried on to school and informed them what had happened. I did carry on to school afterwards, limping like mad and feeling a right idiot.

I was astonished when I got home and Mom opened the door and said straight away, 'What have you been up to then?'

I thought, 'Blimey, she's psychic.' However, it turned out the policeman had been and told her what had happened. The knee did get infected and I had to have further treatment; the cut was so deep I have the scar to this day.

A good memory I have is when we were young is of all us children sitting around the table making paper chains for Christmas and having a good laugh together. This is a lovely memory for me as after that time I was never really close to my stepbrothers. I did keep in touch with my stepsister on and off throughout the years but inevitably our early closeness dwindled and we are no longer in touch with any of my family.

At school, we had to be weighed; the humiliation of having to queue up and stand on a pair of weighing scales; whoever was doing the weighing (normally the gym mistress) would write your weight down in a register whilst shouting it out for all and sundry to hear. Of course, there were quite a few overweight girls in the form, but I was the only one ever picked on when my weight was shouted out. Now, this shaming could have easily been avoided by the gym teacher making a note in her register and moving straight on to the next girl.

Thinking back, I now wonder why they carried this out; if we were overweight, why on Earth didn't they inform our parents? It was such a pointless operation; not of course, as far as the bullies were concerned as it gave them more ammunition to fire at me from the moment the teacher shouted it out.

The Corey family lived not far from where us in Barnsdale Crescent. They lived on the opposite side of the road a little way along. I'm sure there were no girls in the family, just boys. One of the lads was called Brian, I think he was the middle son. Brian was a few years older than me and I remember having a chat to him one day and he told me that he was going in the army to do his National Service; he mentioned that he was being posted to a place called Aden. This meant nothing to me apart from the fact he was going overseas. I offered to write to him and he jumped at the chance. About a month later, I received my first 'bluey' (airmail letter). I was thrilled and sat down immediately to reply. It was simply a good friendship that lasted the whole time Brian served abroad.

When he came home, to my great surprise and excitement he bought me a beautifully embroidered set of blue silk pyjamas, the jacket had a mandarin collar with a matching pair of slippers. I never wore them; I kept them for many years and only wish I could remember what happened to them.

One day Brian Corey, asked me if I would like to go for a ride on his motorbike. I jumped at the chance. It was thrilling; he said he touched a hundred mph as we headed towards Bromsgrove. I loved every exciting moment of it; this was before it was made legal to wear crash helmets, and before motorways cut swathes through the countryside and, of course, there wasn't the amount of traffic on the roads as there is now.

For the first time in our lives, we began to go on holidays and we really enjoyed them; they helped me forget some of the traumas of school life. I used to pretend we were going to stay on at the holiday home and live there so I'd never have to return to that school on the hill. At times, I really hoped Mom would forget me so I could stay and live wherever we happened to be. Despite life improving after I met Hazel, some of the girls still made my life a misery. I never told my parents or even Pauline about the bullying. It is strange to think now that I felt guilty as if it was my fault that those girls were so vile to me. Calling me fatty, four-eyes, smelly, amongst other things. Nowadays there is a lot more help available for the victims of bullying, but I don't think it will ever be stamped out completely.

The first holiday we took was at a place called Arley near Kidderminster. We stayed at a bungalow in the country along with other family members. The men went fishing every day. It was the first time I had been near cows and they seemed so huge to me; I was absolutely terrified. One day I got really terror struck as one was coming right towards me; I ran for my life and escaped into another field only to start sinking in a bog. I screamed and screamed and one of my uncles came to my rescue; he hauled me out and I left one of my red Wellington boots behind. I didn't care I was just so relieved to be out of it. I still can't go into a field of cows, or anywhere near them.

A few years ago, I was at the cottage my mother-in-law owned at that time in Wales. It is set in beautiful countryside near Hereford. I had taken my young granddaughter for a walk to the local church and as we were returning along the lane to the cottage, young Laura happened to glance behind her, and the next thing I heard was a scream and then her shout, 'Run, Nanny, run. There's a cow behind us.' On looking round I saw there was indeed a cow not far away. We took to our heels and didn't stop until we were in the cottage garden and the gate firmly shut. Looking along the lane, I saw that the cow was plodding along without a care in the world, certainly not going as fast as I had thought. I later learnt that a lady who lived on the edge of the moors owned the cow, along with others, and they frequently went walkabout.

We would also go to a caravan site called Edith Mede near to Brean Sands (close to Weston-super-Mare). I can't remember that much about it except I used to go across the field to the farm in the mornings and return with a jug of fresh foaming milk. It was delicious and icy cold, I'm pretty certain you wouldn't be allowed to buy it like that nowadays with all the Health and Safety laws.

I vaguely remember a family holiday spent camping; Pauline was allowed to bring one of her friends along. Her name was Pat Nesbitt; she was a small dark-haired girl who introduced me to the delights of Pan Stick make up that was all the rage then. She and Pauline shared a tent together and I would go over and watch them making up their faces with Pan Stick, lipstick, face powder and then spraying gold spot on their tongues to avoid having bad breath. They also chewed some sweets called sweet violets; at least I think that's what they were called. It was like seeing a whole new world to me and I longed to have a try of the make-up. No joy, I was told politely to go away.

One of the nicest holiday resorts we used to go to was a place called Beesands in Devon. It was wonderful. Whoever said summers were longer and warmer when we were young were right because that's how I recall them, particularly Beesands. It was a golden gleaming place; we would sit on the beach watching the sun slip below the horizon and the fishermen returning with their catch late at night. I think Pauline fell in love with one of the younger fishermen. I just remember it as a beautiful place. We would walk round the cliffs to Hall Sands, which was a deserted village, and I remember the BBC filmed a television programme there a few years later, which brought back some happy memories. Mom used to cook the crab she bought from the fisherman. I'm not going into detail, but the way it was cooked was horrendous. I still shudder when I think about it.

I would play on the sands with the younger members of the family and paddle in the sea. I never learnt to swim; I always had a horror of taking my feet of the ground. Unfortunately, time doesn't stand still and when I returned to Beesands in later years, obviously it had all changed but I could swear I saw the ghosts of two young girls sitting on the beach gazing out to sea.

1955-1960s

When we were fifteen or so, Hazel and I got a Saturday job at Woolworths in the Bull Ring, Birmingham. I worked on the electrical counter.

Management were very strict in those days and you had to tow the line or you were out. I was fortunate in that the lady (Irene) whose counter I worked on was very nice indeed and she soon showed me the ropes. The counter was at the far end of the store and I frequently had to run down a steep flight of stone stairs to the storeroom for items to re-stock the counter. If I couldn't find the item I needed, I had to ask one of the stockroom assistants to help me. One of the assistants became my first boyfriend. His name was John and he came from Saltley. I really fell for him in a big way, and any excuse I could make, I would run down the stairs in the hopes of seeing him. One day he asked me to go to the pictures with him. We were to meet outside the Bristol cinema at seven o'clock.

When the great day arrived, I was full of nerves thinking he wouldn't turn up, or the bus would be late, everything that could possibly go wrong ran through my head. When the time to get ready arrived, I dressed myself up for the date in a gingham skirt Hazel and I had made together with a nice smart blouse, and felt so glamorous. It still surprises me how on a Friday night we would get together and run our weekend clothes up on a small Singer sewing machine. Hazel was the talented one; it took me a long time to conquer sewing.

Waiting for the bus was agony thinking that it might break down, and torturing myself that it would be full and I wouldn't be able to get on it. Of course, the bus arrived on the dot and dropped me off in plenty of time. I looked around and could see no sign of John, but wasn't unduly

36

worried thinking his bus was probably running late. I waited and waited and waited for him and my heart slowly sank to my boots. I could not believe he would stand me up. At just turned seven thirty, I heard someone calling my name. My heart skipped a beat or two as I recognised his voice, 'phew,' was I relieved; John was calling me from across the road. My relief was short-lived as when he crossed over, he started shouting (honest) that he'd been waiting for me for over half an hour on the opposite side of the road. The stupid unforgivable part was that he had been watching me. My infatuation died there and then and I caught the next bus home, vowing never to go out with him or another boy again.

A strange thing happened a couple of days later; a letter dropped on the doormat and Mom looked shocked as she read it and passed it to me without a word. It was from John's mother and she was asking what I was doing going out with her son. For a few minutes, I was lost for words and then I told Mom what had happened when I had gone to meet him. She snatched the letter from me and threw it on the fire. I still puzzle sometimes as to why the woman wrote that letter. What did she think I wanted with her son; after all we were only friends?

Irene, the lady I worked with, asked me about my big night out. When I explained what had happened, she said I'd had a lucky escape and that it was best to find out about him the first night rather than further down the line. 'Mr Right will be along soon enough, you mark my words, me ducks.' She was right of course and my heart healed a little more at her wise words.

On the electrical counter where I worked at Woolworths, you had to test the light bulbs before you sold them; this was quite a hazardous task. To check them we had to screw each bulb into a holder and then switch it on; the bulbs would frequently explode, it's only now I realise how lucky I was never to get the glass in my face. Somehow, I do not think that practice would be allowed today.

I stayed at Woolworths for some time, avoiding the storeroom as much as I could, but eventually I decided a change was called for. Determined to spread my wings, I soon found other employment at George Mason's grocery shop in Rubery. I can still recall the smell of the cheeses and tea; they hit you when you entered the shop! I worked on the cooked meat counter. It was a very busy shop with two facing counters. You could work all day and not speak to the assistants on the other side of the shop because business was always so brisk.

Pauline and I would go off to see our Grandma and Granddad Humphries most weekends. We would catch the bus to Acocks Green and then walk to Thornfield Road. We loved going, they were both so kind to us girls. They would set a small table up in the back garden on summer days and give us a lovely day making a real fuss of us. Arriving one afternoon we knocked on the door, strange, no reply, so we knocked again and then again even louder. We were puzzled because Grandma was always in, then we heard a faint voice calling, 'Go away, go away, I've had a stroke.' There was no way we could get in and see what had happened so we decided to go home. Along the way, we met the next-door neighbour, Mrs Wagstaff, who had called out 'hello' as we were making our way to Grans. She asked us why we were leaving so early and we told her what had happened. To our bewilderment, she rushed off and we made our way home.

Mom was surprised to see us back so early and we explained what had happened. Mom looked worried and just then, Dad arrived home, and we again told our story, and as we finished, he rushed around and then hurried out saying he was off to Acocks Green.

Telephones were not installed in many houses at that time so communication was quite difficult when it came to emergencies. My memory of what happened next is hazy, but I do recall going to see Grandma; she was in a bed that had been brought downstairs as she was so poorly, and sadly she died soon after. Apparently, we moved into Thornfield Road for a few weeks to help Granddad out, and Pauline and I went to the school not far away. I do remember us two girls went home one weekend to dust and tidy round. There was a glass-fronted wall cupboard that had some crockery in it. Pauline stood on a chair, opened the door to the cupboard and was about to dust inside when she screamed, hearing her I looked and joined in the screaming. There were bats flying about. I dislike bats and fluttery creatures; they are okay at a distance but these were too close for comfort. We got out as fast as we could and refused to go again until the bats had gone. I do not think they were a protected species then as they are now, so no doubt Mom and Dad got rid of them, as fortunately we never saw them again.

Mom could cut out and run up a skirt in next to no time. It goes to show that women of her generation were extremely clever at homemaking. I remember Pauline was making a skirt one time with Mom's help. The pattern and material were laid out on the floor when Pauline muttered, 'I need another piece of cloth.' I don't know what happened next but she suddenly shouted, 'Oh what have I done?' It turned out that for some reason or other she had cut her skirt in half. Thank goodness, I was not involved or I would have certainly been in trouble.

Leaving day at school arrived and I was so happy I was fit to burst with excitement; I was more than keen to finish at that place forever, and for once, Hazel and me were early. Even on that day, a couple of the girls had to have a pop at me, but I didn't care; nothing could upset me that day knowing that it was leaving day.

After we had left, it was time to find full-time work. My form mistress, Miss Burrows, had advised me to try for a job in catering, as she knew I loved cooking. She arranged for me to go for an interview at a large restaurant in Birmingham. She even took me in her car. I was offered the job, but Mom said I wasn't to take it as the hours and work in catering were awful, particularly the pay. Sadly, I had to refuse this job; I was disappointed but had to go along with what Mom said. I remember prior to this having to go and see the Career's Officer when she visited the school, she advised me to go and work at Woolworths. When I told Mom she went ballistic, saying that no daughter of hers was going to work full-time in Woolworths. I thought this was very strange, as I had worked in the store for a few years, albeit part-time. Mom seemed to think that having been educated at a Grammar School, it was unseemly to waste the education at Woollies.

The Monday after leaving school, Hazel and I went out looking for work. We walked around Northfield village looking in shop windows for vacancy cards and knocking on office doors. Hazel suggested that we separate as we stood a far better chance of finding work on our own; I could see the sense in this and agreed. I walked to the bottom of the village and noticed a small sign at the side of a chemist's shop. J.C. Morgan's, Quantity Surveyors, it was opposite Smokey Joe's café. I decided to try my luck. I climbed the dark stairwell and found myself on a small dark landing. There was a door to my right and one facing with a step leading up to it. I knocked on the door to my right. The door with the step opened immediately (by now I was quaking in my shoes) and a tall man wearing a dark suit confronted me. He must have been in his forties, though to me he looked quite ancient. Nervously I managed to stutter out my business, he asked me into his office.

After a few questions as to my experience (or rather lack of it), I was ready to leave. Suddenly, he asked me my interests. I mentioned that I went regularly to the Plymouth Brethren Meeting House in St. Heliers Road. (I was at the religious stage of my life). His whole attitude changed then and question followed question. It turned out that his family belonged to the Brethren in Rednal. I was offered a job. He informed me that I would be trained as a comptometer operator and I was also to answer the telephone, make the tea, and do reception duties, and whatever else cropped up. He then showed me around the rest of the offices. There was a passage facing his office, along which were the toilets and a small kitchen. At the end, there was a large room. This was what was known as the boys' room. Mr Morgan quickly introduced me to the five men who were working at their desks, and then took me up to the small office facing his, which was to be where I worked. In the room were two desks, on the one by the window was a small switchboard and typewriter; on the other was a machine known as a comptometer. J.C. Morgan gave me a quick demonstration as to how the telephone system operated and I suddenly realised that a whole new world was going to open up for me. Excited and delighted, I hurried home anxious to tell Mom I was starting work on Monday.

Eric Morgan known as J.C. had also said that the firm would send me to a school in Birmingham City Centre where I would be taught how to use the computer. Almost immediately on starting work, I was sent to the school. Maths had never been my forte and on finishing the course, I was still almost completely in the dark. The whole experience made me feel ill and I had constant stomach pains the whole of the time I was at the school. I was very

41

worried about not being able to understand the course, as I knew if I told J.C., I would almost certainly lose my job. Fortunately, there was so much work at the office that they employed a temporary worker. She was brilliant, took me under her wing, and gave me lessons on how to use the comptometer. I quickly picked up the workings of the machine and after a couple of day's tuition; I was operating the comptometer with confidence as if I had been using it for years. The stomach pains disappeared as fast as they had arrived and I began to eat again without feeling sick. I found using the comptometer very easy and enjoyed adding, subtracting, multiplying, and dividing on it; it was brilliant and I thought if only I had had one at school I would have passed mathematics with ease. I was very grateful to that young woman for her tuition; otherwise, I am quite sure I would have quickly lost my first job. When she had the office sorted, another lady, Mrs Bosanquet, came in part-time to help with the typing when we had a backlog of work.

Mrs Bosanquet was one of the Morgan's relatives, and told me she was related to Reginald Bosanquet, who worked in television. During the lunch hour, she would take out her current embroidery to work on. I remember one she was working was a blue tablecloth, she was covering it in tiny white flowers Mrs Bosanquet called it her snowflake cloth. I was impressed by her talent and told her so, she kindly offered to teach me some of her skills. I had done embroidery from early on but she showed me many different stitches that I didn't know about, and we spent many happy lunch hours stitching and chatting. I have a lot to thank that kind lady for as I have carried on embroidering on and off over the passing years, constantly trying to improve my skills.

My job was answering the telephone and showing visitors in, and any other jobs that came along during the day, but my main job was working on the comptometer. I quickly came to realise what an important job this was as it entailed pricing up the Bills of Lading. The Bills were huge books of pages with jobs listed and priced, and my job was to add each page and eventually reach a final total. It was essential to get that final price correct or the whole job would be wrongly priced and then there would be trouble for someone, namely me. Looking back, I think it was a tremendous responsibility to put on a sixteen-year-old girl fresh out of school with no experience in that type of work whatsoever. I seem to remember I did make a huge mistake once and really got into trouble. I felt so guilty about it for a long time.

The firm did not at that time belong to the man that interviewed me. He was Eric Morgan and I believe he lived at Rednal with his wife and two young children. The firm was his father's; he rarely came into the office, as he was an elderly man. He was a small, smartly dressed man, who I would term a real gentleman of the old school. It was always a pleasure to see him when he paid us a visit.

I remember Eric Morgan hated flies and even when it was eighty degrees Fahrenheit outside, he would sit locked in his office (this overlooked the Bristol Road) lest any demon fly should get in. He always wore a full suit and waistcoat and never took his jacket off at work. One of the 'boys' told me that even on holiday he dressed the same. He told me that he saw the younger Morgan family on the beach abroad one summer day, and Eric Morgan had his suit on sitting under an umbrella fanning himself.

During my stay at Morgan's the younger Mr Morgan asked me if I would go to the church where he worshipped one Sunday evening and give a talk to the congregation on how I was 'saved'. I agreed and wrote out a short testament and duly stood up in front of a small congregation at the church in Rednal and read my notes. On remembering this,

I now wonder at my courage because I am far from an outgoing person, and always refuse offers to give talks when asked.

I did enjoy my work coping with the running of the office and never felt lonely when on my own. It was nice when Mrs Bosanquet came in, but I did like doing the various jobs that cropped up through the day.

I was surprised one Monday morning when young Mr Morgan said he was interviewing women that day for the position of a typist. I never discovered what had happened to his previous employees. He took on a woman named Jean who lived in Cotteridge. She was a woman in her mid-forties who lived at home taking care of her elderly mother. She travelled into Northfield on the number 27 bus. The first thing I noticed about her was she was wearing a very heavy silver charm bracelet, it was absolutely jam-packed with charms, and I can recall thinking how strong she must have been, as it certainly looked very heavy.

The first couple of weeks everything was fine, and we seemed to get on quite well. Then one day she said we should exchange places, as she should answer the switchboard. Her reason was that it interfered with my figure work. I was dumbstruck. I enjoyed answering the calls. She also said she was going to show visitors in as well. Apparently, she had discussed this with Mr Morgan and he was in full agreement. I didn't have a leg to stand on, demoted was the way I saw it and things were never the same after that. Answering the phone and seeing the visitors had taken some of the monotony out of the figure work and given me a break. Apart from which, I was very hurt to think that I had coped for nearly twelve months on my own and then they had gone behind my back, taking on someone new and over all made me feel pretty useless.

The firm also operated a bonus system; and of course, after I was demoted to junior I received next to nothing and that didn't sit easy after all my hard work in sorting the office out.

After a few months, I found another job and left J.C. Morgan's. My new job was in Birmingham City Centre at the GPO where I was employed as a typist. My job was typing forms to do with people who were being prosecuted for not having a television/wireless license. Despite enjoying working in the City Centre, I didn't like working in such a large office. Morgan's had been a small friendly place to work (at first) and I felt utterly lost in this vast building. I persevered for a while, but soon found another job in Selly Oak. (Work was easy to find in those times).This job entailed working out customer accounts for Radio Rentals on a machine. Considering I was hopeless at Maths, it amazed me how I kept finding jobs that involved figure work. Again though, I found myself unsettled, once more working in a large office, and wondered what I should do.

A couple of months later, my sister Pauline said there was a job going at Ten Acres & Stirchley Cooperative Society in Stirchley where she worked. She offered to get me an interview. I jumped at the chance and was soon on my way to TASCOS. I wasn't very hopeful as the position was for a secretary with shorthand and typing skills. I could type but certainly not first class, and had no knowledge of shorthand, but was more than willing to learn. Hazel seems to remember we went to Bournville School for evening classes to learn typing but I cannot remember doing that. To my great surprise, I got the job. What was more, they were willing to train me in shorthand and help brush up my typing skills.

Early 1960s

I was to work for Alderman Sidney Watts - who was a member of Birmingham City Council - in the Credit Sales Office. It was a busy office. There was much to-ing and fro-ing as club collectors came and went throughout the day.

I never had anything to do with the collectors as Sid Watts was in charge of that department, and the head of the club collectors was Mr Wilkes.

He was a very nice man who unfortunately suffered from stomach ulcers, and from time to time he looked very ill, almost gaunt. I put it down to the stress of his job as there were many club collectors and he held a very important job, plus he took his work very seriously.

My job was checking customer hire purchase accounts and if they were going into arrears, I would send out a polite reminder to bring their payment up to date. If this failed, a further letter was sent; if no payment was forthcoming, then a third letter threatened court action.

I also checked new applications for credit worthiness and then typed up the agreements, answered the telephone, and interviewed customers who called into reception.

The Co-op sent me for lessons in shorthand and typing to a woman who lived in Cartland Road, Stirchley. I went on a Wednesday afternoon for a couple of hours when the offices were closed. Despite being very strict, the lady was a good teacher and I quickly grasped the basics; within six months I was taking down letters, albeit slowly, but with only a few mistakes.

Sid Watts told me that if I learned shorthand within twelve months, I would have a good pay rise. Well, I learnt within nine months and was given the princely increase of two shillings and also an extra two shillings (ten pence in new money) for being in charge of the office and running it when he was absent.

I really enjoyed my job. There were two other girls, one was Christine Workman, her mother was a small plump pleasant lady who quite often popped into reception, she worked as a supervisor in one of the offices at Cadbury's Bourneville that was just around the corner. Rosemary, whose last name I have forgotten, was the other girl who worked alongside us, and also Gladys Trower, who came in part-time to help with the typing. Later on, a young girl by the name of Diane Bowmaster joined our small team as office junior.

Sid went out and about on various civic duties and we girls made the most of it and had a good many enjoyable times in his absence. Not that he was a bad boss by any means, he was very fair-minded, but he frowned on chitchat during working time. It could have been a heavy atmosphere to work in, but my job entailed quite a few walkabouts throughout the course of the day, taking me into other offices where the girls were allowed to have a friendly chat.

Gladys Trower was quite a remarkable lady. Prior to working in our office, she had worked in the typing pool upstairs. She was a married lady, her husband was called Reg, they had no children. One year the couple went on holiday to Switzerland and Gladys suffered a severe stroke; I seem to remember her saying it was touch and go for a time. She could not have been very old at the time. Fortunately, for her, she made an excellent recovery. In fact, the illness seemed to give her a new lease of life. She lost a tremendous amount of weight and her energy levels were something to be seen. She hardly ever seemed to sit still except to do her typing, which she did at tremendous speed; it was impressive to watch her.

From the time she entered the office after lunch, she was like a small whirlwind with every part of her body energised; you could almost see her brain working. She really impressed me, and best of all, she had a wonderful sense of humour.

One thing that sticks in my mind and always makes me smile whenever I remember it; every year we had a small Christmas tree in the office prior to the Christmas break, and we decorated it with the usual glass baubles and glittery stuff, we all enjoyed dressing it up. This particular year, Gladys had been too busy to buy one, so she asked Sid Watts if she could 'borrow' the office tree plus decorations. Sid agreed and when work finished for the day, off she trotted with the tree as happy as one of Santa's little helpers. I watched her walking down Pershore Road towards home smiling happily carrying the tree. True to her word, she returned the decorations.

In fact, I still have one of the old Chinese lanterns that I 'borrowed' one year, for some reason it never was returned.

Rosemary was a very quiet efficient young girl who didn't stay with us very long; unfortunately, I never got to know her very well. Diane took her place. I was a few years older than Diane was, but we became good friends. After she met Robert Tyler, who was later to become her husband, we would all go out and about together and have some good times.

As far as I know, Christine Workman had always worked at the Co-op since leaving school; she was an only child and had a strong sense of family. Christine and her fiancé built their first home along with others on a self-build scheme. It must have been one of the first schemes of its kind in the Birmingham area.

TASCOS Co-op was a vast building on the corner of Umberslade Road. The radio and chemist shops were on the opposite corner. In the rooms above the chemist was the staff canteen. We visited the canteen three times a day. I would meet up with Pauline and the girls from the typists' office from upstairs every morning and we would walk across for our breaks together. It was subsidised by the company so it was very cheap. The teacakes were delicious, as were the dinners. Rain or shine, sleet, fog or snow, we never missed a break.

Sid Watts owned a caravan at a small caravan site about two miles from Harlech. He offered me the use of it and I jumped at the chance. At the time, I was going out with a boy called Bob who worked at the GPO (General Post Office) as a counter clerk in Northfield. Bob and I had in fact being going out together for a few years. We decided to take Sid up on his offer and go for a week.

I booked the coach that would take us from Digbeth Coach Station to Barmouth, and was told that we could catch a bus to the caravan site, as it was quite a way out of Barmouth. I was really excited and looked forward to our break.

The great day arrived and Bob and I set off for Birmingham, we realised that we were running a little late as we struggled across town with our luggage, but thought we would be okay for time. Hurrying down the hill towards the coach station, we couldn't believe our eyes as we saw our coach heading off. Bob jumped up and down flapping his arms and shouting, no good came of it though, the coach went off in a cloud of dust leaving two dispirited holidaymakers (well, hoping to be,) in the lurch. We asked around and found to our dismay that it was the only coach to Barmouth that weekend. We toiled back up the hill obviously very downhearted when Bob suggested we take the train. What a good idea, I thought, and off we trotted to New Street Station. We were both delighted when we found there was a train going to Barmouth and we were so

49

relieved when we finally took our seats. We both felt complete idiots and promised each other not to tell anyone we'd managed to miss the coach. Of course, we eventually told everyone and had a good laugh about it.

There was worse to come though when we eventually arrived at Barmouth, we were dumbfounded to find there wasn't a bus to the caravan site until the following week. What could we do now, we wondered? There was only one thing for it; we would have to walk. It was a long walk of about eight miles in all, with our luggage to carry as well. We were both exhausted when we finally arrived and fortunately managed to buy some milk and food from the site shop just to tide us over until the Sunday. After such a disastrous start, we wondered what else could possibly go wrong, but fortunately, nothing did and we had quite an enjoyable holiday. When the time came to leave, we made certain we allowed extra time to catch the coach home. Quite a few of the returning passengers remarked, 'Oh so you're the two who missed the coach.' Pretty obvious really, I thought.

It all seemed so easy then to meet up and go on a treasure hunt or just a walk around the nearby country lanes or the Lickey Hills. On a summer weekend, the queue at the bus terminus at Rednal would wind itself round and round as whole families made their way home. There was a small indoor fair and a few slot machines a place to buy ice cream, and other things; everybody seemed to have a good day out. People would go bilberry picking up the hills and come back with dark stains around their lips. I cannot ever remember feeling frightened that someone would attack or rob me, but then I was an innocent. Bob asked me to marry him and I was bowled over. I really thought he was the man for me and was delighted to accept his offer. One evening, he told me to wait in the porch of 43, Barnsdale Crescent while he went in to ask my parents if they would let him marry me. What a nice man he was. They said yes, of course, and we were both happy that they had agreed.

Bob worked as a counter assistant at Northfield Post Office. I only ever met his mother once; looking back this seems quite strange as we went out together for quite a while. Hazel, my friend from school days, was going out with a young man called Les Robinson, and we often all got together for a night out to the pictures or a walk along Merritt's Brook. Bob took me into The Bell Inn once but I wasn't very keen; neither of us were drinkers.

The four of us decided to go on holiday together, so one Saturday, Hazel and I squeezed into the small sidecar of Les' motorbike, with all the pots and pans hanging on the outside. Off we went to the Lake District. We made camp in a field just after dark. Having put the tents up, we retired to bed only to wake up in the morning to find a herd of cows surrounding our camp. Being a city girl at heart, I was very wary of the cows and fled across the field in terror, leaving the others to pack up. We made camp on a proper campsite afterwards. I decided to perm my hair, but why I did it I'll never know, as I had naturally curly hair. Anyway, there I was, neutralizing and rinsing my hair in the middle of a wet soggy field. The end result was dreadful as my hair went dead straight and has remained straighter than a poker ever since

The holiday did me good as I lost over a stone in weight!

What fun we all had on our holidays. Hazel and I shared the 'big tent' and the boys had a small tent each.

The 'big tent' was in fact an old army tent, and we had to put an empty bean can on the top to anchor it down. Well, that is what the boys said, but I never understood why. Strange how your memory fades as you grow older, all I can remember of that holiday was the laughs we had. We all got on famously and shared the chores between us.

The record *Bobby's Girl* by Susan Maughan became a hit single and my brothers took every opportunity to torment me so much, I came to loathe it. Whenever I hear it played now I'm whisked back to Barnsdale Crescent, where we're all sitting round the table and my brothers are tormenting me rotten with that song. I hated them for taking the mickey out of me.

We left Northfield and moved to Redditch in 1962 and unfortunately for me, as with school, I was usually late for work. Our father would drop us at The Man in the Moon Public House at West Heath, then we had to rely on the bus service. The trouble was the bus was often late or never arrived. As it was my job to open the large double doors for customers and workers to come in at 8.30 a.m. when I was late I would get into trouble with Mr Watts and received numerous warnings. We closed between 12.30 p.m. to 1.30 p.m. and the office day ended at 5 p.m.

One morning, Sid Watts rushed off to attend a meeting in Birmingham. Smoking was frowned on in our office. Mr Watts didn't smoke and neither did Gladys; she only worked afternoons as a rule so as soon as he'd left the office, out came the 'fags' and we lit up. Suddenly, the door sprang open and in rushed Mr Watts. My ashtray was in my desk drawer so I quickly dropped my cigarette into it and slammed the drawer shut, saying a prayer that he'd leave very soon. I quickly started typing as the smoke wafted gently through the slit in the drawer; my heart was in my mouth praying he wouldn't notice. He never said a word as I tried desperately to keep a straight face. He grabbed his diary and almost ran out of the office, much to my relief.

To my knowledge, Sid Watts never married. I know he had brothers, I think one of them was called Ralph, who ran a butcher's shop. Sid lived with his mother and looked after a young girl; she was called Christine, and was about eight or nine when I knew her. After I married, Sid would bring her to tea at my flat, or we would take her out and about with us. I don't know whether he was fostering the young girl or had actually adopted her.

One afternoon, there was only Sid and myself in the office when quite out of the blue, he said, 'You know, Carol, I think that when you die, you become a small light that stays in space for eternity.' I thought this was a very strange thought to drop on someone during the course of the afternoon so I just agreed with him. A few years after I had left Birmingham, I heard that he had died suddenly of a heart attack. I was saddened because he did excellent work for the City of Birmingham, and I know for certain he did a lot of charity work. He was a thoroughly nice man.

I will never forget the day I was showing the girls my new bottle of perfume. It was a bottle of Chanel No. 5. It was beautiful and they crowded round to have a dab put on their wrists, All of a sudden, the bottle slipped through my fingers and shattered on the office floor. I was mortified and it was many years before I was treated to a new bottle. Needless to say, the office smelt wonderful for a long time.

One day, Pauline told me she was going to the hairdressers to have her beautiful long hair cut short. I was surprised to say the least as everyone admired her hair. It was her pride and joy. The hairdressing salon was downstairs in the Co-op Shop. She asked if I would meet her outside the pub across the road at about one o'clock. I could not believe she was going to do it and begged her not to go. I couldn't change her mind and waited in trepidation for her, knowing she would hate it. On seeing her, I thought it looked okay, but it was a dramatic change. She never said a word, just sat down beside me with her head bowed. I did tell her it looked nice, but she sat quite still for a few minutes then the tears started to fall. I put a comforting arm around her and told her to dry her eyes, as after all it would grow back very quickly. She then told me she felt suicidal and that really worried me. I worried that she was depressed enough to do it as well. Fortunately, she didn't and her hair grew back in time.

Pauline had beautiful nails and I always admired them, she really looked after them. I was always impressed at how she managed to keep them so long as she did a tremendous amount of typing, but when it came to cutting them she is the only adult I have ever known who cried when she had to cut them. She always said it was so painful that she couldn't help but cry.

I always have to smile when I remember the following incident. When we lived in Northfield and were both working for the Co-op. one morning Pauline shook me awake saying, 'Come on, come on, Carol, we're going to be late for work.' It was quite a dark morning, I thought to myself waiting at the bus stop and not many people around at all, but as I wasn't fully awake, I followed Pauline's lead as per usual. It dawned on us when we got to Cotteridge that we were about three hours too early for the bus to work. We quickly and quietly made our way home! That took some living down at home and at work when we were found out.

Pauline had a brilliant job. She was secretary to Mr Lee; he was deputy to the managing director, Mr Grainger. Pauline was also secretary to Gwen Hurley, who in turn was in charge of the typists' pool and secretary to Mr Grainger.

The typists' pool was situated on the first floor; it was the first office at the top of the stairs. Visitors had to tap on the small hatch that faced the stairs and one of the girls would attend to them. It was normally Mrs Danks who looked after the visitors; she was a small slim lady and was one of Pauline's best friends. I really liked her and in all the years I knew her, she never said a word against anyone she knew; truly a lovely lady.

Gwen Hurley's desk was on a small raised platform and her staff sat in rows of three in front of her. The more senior staff was situated immediately in front of her. Pauline, Mrs Danks, and Audrey Trower made up the first row as far as I remember.

Audrey was a nice woman. One of her daughters, Shirley, worked for a short while in the typist's office. Shirley was a beautiful young woman, all dark long curly hair, and beautiful. She didn't stay long as she was of a very nervous disposition and the typists' office was no place for someone of a gentle nature like Shirley. Audrey was Gladys Trower's sister in law.

Gwen was extremely strict and commanded a lot of respect. I never understood how Pauline managed to get along with her, but then Pauline was a much stronger character than I was.

I remember one of the other girls was named Gail, and there was also Ann Bagnall, but all the other girl's names escape me. Mind you, it was a long time ago!

On the first floor to the right of the passage, facing the typist's office was a door that led into an empty room. Quickly passing through this room you entered another one. This was a fascinating room to me as it housed the main telephone switchboard for the whole of the Co-op. It made my five-line switchboard at Morgan's look miniscule. This was a plug in/out board and it was massive. Lillian was the person in charge of it, and another woman helped her to operate it. I would gaze in wonder as they answered calls whilst connecting and disconnecting callers. I always longed to have a go, but never had the courage to ask.

Lillian was a small disabled woman with lovely brunette hair, she had a wonderful sense of humour, and I spent many a pleasant hour with her cracking jokes and watching her work.

Mr Lee's office was next along the passage and then Mr Grainger's, then once past the big boss's office, there was a spiral staircase that took you down to the bank counter. I didn't use this way very often, as I didn't want to run into any of the higher-ups.

I rarely had to go into the directors' offices but when I did, I noticed that they always only had one document on their highly polished desks, never anything else apart from the telephones.

Gwen and Pauline had to attend committee meetings on a regular basis to take the minutes. About eighteen months after I had been working there, Gwen Hurley asked me to train as a committee clerk. I attended a couple of meetings to see how I got on and presented my reports to Gwen Hurley with trepidation. As I said, Gwen was a hard taskmaster, but to my surprise she sent word back that she was more than pleased with my work and invited me to attend regular meetings and take notes. I thought about this for a while and eventually refused. There was a lot going on in my life at that time and I didn't want to add more work to it.

I also worked Saturday afternoons in the Radio and Television Shop across the road from the offices. Business was very brisk during the years I worked at TASCOS. In the week, I would check the credit worthiness of customers who I had helped sell a washing machine or television to on a Saturday, then check the agreement in the office the following week and type it up ready for signing. So after giving Gwen Hurley's offer a lot of thought, I decided against it.

I was invited to one of the cocktail parties that the directors held. I only really knew Pauline and Gwen so I kept close to them during the evening. One of the directors approached us with a packet of cigarettes and proffered them to Pauline, who refused, as she didn't smoke. Gwen if

I remember correctly did and she accepted one, the director looked at me and put the packet away! My position was far too lowly to have a ciggy offered. He need not have worried anyway as I didn't smoke at that time; I was too busy trying to save money towards our wedding. Not that I wasn't hurt, I was, but I certainly didn't show it. That was another reason why I refused the job; if I was so low down the scale of things in that director's eye, I certainly wasn't going to sit in the same room as him taking notes.

Pauline was always smartly dressed. Whatever she wore, she had the ability to make it look good. If she was wearing a plain blouse, she would add a snazzy silk scarf and immediately it looked right with her straight dark skirt and stiletto-heeled shoes. Pauline wore nice jackets to compliment her outfits, and with her beautiful long hair always backcombed into the latest fashion, she was a very stylish woman. In fact, her hair was something else. How she managed to backcomb it so high was quite something. It never moved even if the wind was gale force, she would use nearly a whole bottle of lacquer on it to keep it in place. It was truly a remarkable sight. How Pauline managed to keep using the amount of hair lacquer that she did was beyond me. The slightest amount made my head itch like crazy.

I don't think the Beehive style will ever make a real comeback but if it did, it would certainly cause a stir.

One day I decided I wanted the latest look so off I went to the Co-op hairdressers in the shop basement. The leading stylist was a man called Phillip and he gave me the kitten style, he said it was all the rage. My new hairdo was greatly admired and the next day was still as good as new, though stiff as a board and itching like mad from the lacquer. I had to keep myself cool so that the itching was kept to a minimum. That morning Pauline and I were travelling into work on the bus when the conductor came to take our fares. He made a point of catching my eye and then to my utter astonishment, he asked me to marry him. He was quite a young man, very nice-looking, but I didn't know him from Adam. I stuttered, 'Pardon?' He repeated his offer.

Pauline poked me in the ribs and we both started laughing until he said, 'I am quite serious, you know.' That wiped the grin off my face and I looked out of the window very embarrassed. To my relief and probably his, I never saw him again. Fashion wise I was different to Pauline. Of course, I dressed smartly for work, but I went for the more casual look when I was able. Pauline always wore stiletto heels and kept her hair backcombed to the hilt to give her added height. That was one of her groans that she wasn't very tall. She was about five feet one inch. I haven't gone fully metric yet so I cannot convert it! I remember many years later when we were both older and Pauline lived in Scotland, she rang me saying, 'Carol, I've come down to Earth.'

'What do you mean?' I asked puzzled.

'I've binned my high heels for ever!' she exclaimed. 'I got rid of the car and now walk everywhere in my flatties!' I had to laugh at her.

One of her major groans was her weight. She would ring me on the internal phone at work shrieking down the line, 'Carol, I've just measured my backside on my chair and I've put on half an inch.' Gosh she was funny at times and if Sid was sitting at his desk I didn't know what to say as the phones were on his desk and he was always listening. I would hmm and ah, until Pauline realised he was there and she would shout, 'See you at break, Carol.'

One day that sticks in my memory is when Dad was going into Birmingham he dropped Pauline and me off along the Pershore Road not far from Umberslade Road. I got out first and was happily walking off when I realised

Pauline wasn't beside me. I glanced back and was horrified to see her banging the car window and crying and screaming, 'Stop the car, stop the car.' Her thumb was jammed in the car door, and she was running alongside it. Dad stopped and opened the door for her as quickly as he could. My poor sister, her thumb was such a mess it was quite awful to see. Dad offered to take her to Selly Oak Hospital but she refused and we hurried across the road into work. She refused all treatment and despite the pain, she carried on working. Her thumb never regained its shape. For all her small stature, she more than made up for it with her indomitable character. I was so lucky to have her for a sister and friend.

Sid would rarely answer the phone, be it the outside line ringing or the internal one. If Christine wasn't in the office to answer it, I would have to jump up and walk round Sid, who was sitting on his chair, to pick the phone up. I am sure he played little games at times as just as I got round him, he would say, 'It's okay, Carol, I'll get it.' My language in my head was not very ladylike.

I recall one day Mr Watts came rushing back into the office from some mission or other, he hurried to sit down on his chair, missed the seat, and fell sprawling on the floor. I remember trying not to laugh and thinking, 'What's he doing down there?'

I first met John as I was going into work one morning - the office staff used the back door to the Co-op building in Umberslade Road unless you were late, then you ran through the large front doors if, of course, I had managed to scrape in on time to open them. John was repairing a milk float near to the back door, I heard someone give a very loud wolf whistle and looked round, and my first sight of him was a face peering round the back of the vehicle at me. I noticed his very blue eyes and fell head over heels in love. This was no way for a girl who was engaged to another man to feel, but I could not get him out of my mind. Every time we 'accidentally' met after that, my heart would do far too many flutters for a girl who was engaged to someone else. In the end, I knew I had to finish with Bob. That hurt as he was a lovely chap, but not for me. I felt awful about it, but realised it would have been wrong to marry him feeling as I did about John.

I heard a few years ago that he was married and settled with a family. I hope he has fulfilled all his dreams, as he was a smashing man, in fact, as I have said, he was a real gentleman.

John and I got on like a house on fire. We spent every spare minute together going ice-skating at Summer Row Ice Rink in Birmingham. That was a whole new experience for me. John even made me a dress suitable for skating. It was beautiful; red material and had box pleats for the skirt. All in all, it looked very professional, unlike my ice-skating, which I never really found the balance for.

We also went to the pictures and went out walking; we never visited pubs as neither of us enjoyed alcohol that much.

One evening we were in the kitchen at my parents' home and I decided to make us all a cup of tea – all being John, Stephen, Peter, and Jane, my brothers and sister who were at home at the time. Dennis, my eldest brother, and Pauline were out. I put my knitting on the kitchen chair and whilst making the tea, I heard a loud groan and was horrified to see Stephen, who was about 14 at the time, go as white as a sheet as he fainted clean away. He hadn't noticed my knitting on the chair and had sat on one of the needles. I was mortified and John removed the needle; thank goodness, Stephen made a very quick recovery, but I learnt a lesson that night that I have never forgotten.

Mom was washing up late one winter's evening not long after moving into Tennyson Road, she happened to glance up from her task and let out such a scream. I jumped out of my skin as I heard her shouting, 'Go away, go on clear off.' I quickly made my way into the kitchen where Mom told me that an old man had been staring in the window at her. At that time, the garden was still a mass of bricks and rubbish left there by the builders. After that, Dad very quickly got the garden fenced in.

The previous story reminded me of something that happened years later when we lived in Leathermill Lane. Our garden backed onto what was then Celcon's factory. One day I was putting clothes away into the wardrobe that was next to the window that looked out across to Celcon's. I suddenly had the feeling that someone was watching me. I felt a crawling sensation along my arms, up my neck, and into my head. I looked out of the window out of the corner of my eye and saw an old man standing behind the fence staring at me. I quickly looked away and then looked back; he was still watching me. I felt quite sick and moved away as fast as I could. My friends told me that I should have rung the factory, but what could I have accused him of? Still, it left a bad taste in my mouth for a long time afterwards.

One night, John came to Redditch to see me; my parents were out when there was a sudden knock at the door. Wondering who it could be I hurried to the front door where I was greeted by a man, who said, 'Do you know your car is down the bottom of the road?' I mean, as if? I stepped outside and was horrified to see John's parents' car at the bottom of the hill. John had parked directly outside the house instead of parking in the side road that ran alongside the house. We were very fortunate that no one was injured and hardly any damage was caused to property or the car.

The above story reminds me of when John went to the cottage in Colva in Herefordshire that his parents owned, one winter. I have a feeling it was the bad winter of 1963 when the hedgerows were piled high with snow and roads were impassable at times. John was travelling along one of the lanes when all of a sudden he found himself facing in the opposite direction to the way he had been going. The ice was so thick and slippery to say the least.

We babysat for my parents and made plans for our forthcoming wedding; we had got engaged within three months of meeting and then immediately started making our wedding plans. Deciding where to live was a bit difficult, and John's parents suggested John's grandmother's house as she lived on her own and never used the upstairs because she suffered from rheumatics. Her house was in Warwards Lane, Selly Oak. We spent many happy hours converting the back bedroom into a kitchen, the front bedroom in to a lounge and the room along the passageway became our bedroom. There was no bathroom, just a toilet outside in the yard, boring but we managed. We acquired a tin bath that we discovered leaked when we began to fill it with water. What fun we had then, plugging the holes as best we could and standing the bath on lots of newspapers to sop up the water, well, we didn't want Granny to get wet, should it leak through the floorboards.

We furnished the flat on a shoestring budget, buying furniture from second-hand shops; friends and relatives also gave us various articles. We were so happy; it seemed as if we had the world at our feet in those days. While we were converting the flat, we had to take some of the floorboards up in what was going to be our lounge. We always made a point of locking the door in case John's Gran did decide she was fit enough to go upstairs. We worried in case she should trip over the floorboard and hurt herself.

One night we decided to treat ourselves and went to the pictures, when we came out there was a real pea souper of a fog. Knowing there was no way we could get back to Redditch let alone Headless Cross that night, we decided to go to the flat despite there being nothing there in the way of furniture and fittings. Of course, it was pitch black in the house. John opened the lounge door; I followed, and promptly fell through the space where the floorboards should have been. My toe was unbelievably painful that night; not only was I freezing cold, my poor toe throbbed unmercifully. I piled coats, curtains, anything I could find on top of me but could not get warm. I hobbled to work the next morning looking and feeling a real fright, wearing the clothes I had slept in and not even having had a cup of tea.

I carried on working for a couple of days, but one morning I could hardly walk and Sid Watts suggested I go to Casualty at Selly Oak Hospital; he rang John, who came to the office and dropped me off at Casualty. After an X-ray I had my toe put in plaster and was told to go home and rest. They did offer to take me home in an ambulance, but I refused. I rang John and he came and took me home. I missed a couple of weeks of work and was glad when I could go back I really loved my job.

I have good cause to be grateful to Selly Oak Hospital, as when I was twenty my wisdom teeth started to grow inwards, and were extremely painful. I carried on working as you do thinking everything would sort itself out, instead I began to feel ill. We went to Blackpool one weekend with our friends, Hazel and Les. I tried my hardest to enter into the spirit of the weekend, but the pain in my head and jaw became steadily worse and I was having trouble getting about. Travelling home was a real nightmare as we ran into fog all the way home. The next day at work, my face was swollen and I seemed to have lost my entire

63

colour, in fact there were huge dark circles under my eyes and as the day progressed, my face developed a green hue. Sid Watts took over and rang John, suggesting he run me up to the Dental Department at Selly Oak. They were very kind and examined my teeth and the dentist stared hard at me and asked me how I felt. I replied quite honestly that I felt as if I was dying. I mentioned I'd visited the doctor a couple of days earlier and he had given me some iron tablets. The dentist sent me for blood tests and made an appointment for me to return in a couple of days. Still I struggled in the next day, feeling even worse; walking a few steps was becoming a problem, as I was so weak and breathless. Sid Watts must have felt sorry for me as every time the phone rang that morning, he answered it. At about 11.30 a.m., he took another call and hanging up he turned to me and said, 'Carol that was the hospital they want you up there now.' One thing about Sid was he never hung about, as I went even paler, if possible, he picked the phone up and summoned John again, who promptly carted me off to the hospital. Not to the Dental Department, this time, but to see a Dr Nussey, who immediately arranged to admit me, as it appeared the blood tests revealed I had only a third of the iron I needed in my blood.

How I got so anaemic I will never know, but I will be grateful forever to the dentist who arranged for the blood tests that led to my being helped by Dr Nussey and his team. I spent a fortnight in hospital having iron injections and all sorts of other tests, until my blood level showed the correct amount of iron.

As I began to feel better, the nurses would tease John and I when he visited me. They would rush up to us and draw the curtains around the bed, running off giggling amongst themselves. Of course, Sister was not around when this happened; it was all in good fun and brightened the day up.

I was so glad to feel strong again on leaving the hospital; I could walk properly without getting breathless; my skin colour returned to normal, it was good to feel alive again.

The lady in the next bed had been a nurse and she said she really thought I had leukaemia when she first saw me. I am glad she kept that thought to herself, or I would probably have died on the spot as I felt so weak and ill.

John and I rarely ran into each other at the canteen because at that time a class system operated whereby office staff were forbidden to eat with the works people in the staff canteen. There was a large hatch either side of the canteen kitchen and we would give each other a wave at lunchtimes, and then meet up after work.

Eventually to my relief, management changed the rules so John and his friend Reg joined Pauline and me for lunch. I can still see us all now laughing and joking round the canteen table next to the window that looked out onto the busy Pershore Road; they were such happy days.

Pauline was married by this time to a man called Peter Flynn, who was an electrician in the works department at TASCOS. Unfortunately for them, Peter was made redundant when they returned from honeymoon, but he soon got fixed up with another job. They had a flat in Selly Oak for a short while before moving out to Masefield Drive, Tamworth. Pauline then had various jobs in Birmingham. Unfortunately, the marriage didn't work out and they eventually divorced.

I married John at St. Luke's Church in Headless Cross, Redditch on 21st March 1964, Pauline was my chief bridesmaid (Matron-of-honour) Joy, John's sister, was second bridesmaid, and Jane, my youngest sister, was the flower girl. I bought my wedding dress from a shop in Birmingham City Centre. It was made of a beautiful satin material with teardrop crystals hanging from the bodice. I was going to have one made by a woman called Mrs Page who worked in the ladies wear at TASCOS. She was a small, bright as a button lady who made wonderful clothes; we had in fact chatted about my wedding dress, but when I saw this particular one in town, I just had to have it. The bridesmaids were dressed in pink. I organised flowers for them to wear in their hair as each of them had long hair; I envied them. Just before the wedding, they all had their hair cut! It was too late to change the flowers and John and I were on quite a tight budget having to pay for everything. Even the guest list had to be shorter than we wanted, but we could only do so much.

My bouquet was made up of roses and freesias, and Jane held a small pretty basket of flowers

A few days before the wedding, Jane, my young sister, was playing at the local recreation ground in Headless Cross when unfortunately she had an accident and knocked her front teeth out; this is why she looks so serious in our wedding photographs. When I was walking up the aisle with my father, I heard John's Aunty Enid say in a very loud hoarse whisper, 'I much prefer a good funeral to a wedding any day.' It made me smile and I heard a few muffled giggles from the church.

The vicar who was going to marry us took leave the week before the wedding and another vicar held the ceremony. To our dismay, he smelt very strongly of drink and slurred his words, the worst being when he said, 'With this wing I thee wed.' If he hadn't been so serious, it would have been funny. It was a bit like one of Dave Allen's comedy sketches.

We held our reception over at a nice public house out Bromsgrove way. A woman who used to work in TASCOS electrical shop in Stirchley managed the pub; her name was Mavis.

Well, as neither of our families knew each other they sort of lined up each side of the room and never the twain did meet; I think it was more a case of you speak first, but no one did so no one mixed.

Poor Mavis sliced her thumb; it happened halfway through the buffet meal and her husband took her straight off to hospital. I never saw her again.

We had ordered what I thought would be a beautiful three-tier wedding cake, but unfortunately it had a tilt to it and looked like the Leaning Tower of Pisa. Still I thought, it's only a cake at the end of the day and it tasted nice.

Overall, we were glad when it was time to go and change, and get ready to leave for our honeymoon. I had bought a beautiful white fitted dress, it was made of heavy white lace, and I wish I still had it. I bought it from a local dress shop along the Pershore Road; I cannot remember the name of the shop, but you crossed over Umberslade Road and not far along, the shop lay back from the road along with two or three other shops.

Leaving for our honeymoon we said our goodbyes and drove off into the sunset just as a heavy storm blew up from out of nowhere, I always remember thinking, 'I hope this isn't a sign of things to come.'

We stayed at Brookside, a small cottage on the edge of the moors in Wales; a stream runs at the bottom of the garden. It is an idyllic spot. At that time, John's aunt owned it along with another cottage called Glandwr, also situated on the moors. Glandwr was just a shell at that time and John and one of his friends had spent time re-wiring it. I loved both the cottages and could have happily settled in either, but financially that wouldn't have been possible.

One day we sat outside Brookside looking towards the snow-capped mountains and we marvelled how mild it was for the end of March, the sun was shining brightly and, briefly, the world seemed a place of magic and mystery.

The views around the area were quite startling and I was loath to leave the peace and quiet, but after the first week, we moved on to Aberystwyth.

We stayed at a bed and breakfast boarding house and it was quite obvious to all that we were newly married; I think we had that special glow that all newlyweds have. Returning from our honeymoon, I had thirty shillings left (£1.50) to last a week. I really didn't care because we were standing on the threshold of a new life eager and ready to step into the future.

Diane and Robert came to our wedding and we kept in close touch over the years. Diane eventually left the Co-op and went to work for Biddle and Webb Antique Dealers and Auctioneers in Birmingham. She had a good job and often went across to France on business for the company.

Robert worked as an accountant for Charter Homes. When they married, they bought a house at Elford not far from where we eventually came to live in Staffordshire, and we visited each other frequently.

They also came on holiday with us and we shared many happy times together. Eventually we lost touch with our friends to my regret. I did try to trace Diane a couple of years ago and found to my dismay that she and Robert had divorced. I managed to get in touch with her, but again fate stepped in and I lost her new address. I couldn't believe my bad luck having found her again after all those years, and then immediately losing her new telephone number, I know at that time she lived in the Cotswolds with her new family.

Hazel and Les also had a flat in Selly Oak and after I married, we would visit each other for Sunday tea and a good old chat, but unfortunately, as the years passed we eventually lost touch with them. It was only by chance that after twenty years or so, we got in touch with each other. It took quite a while to catch up on the intervening years.

I used to love walking around the Co-op shop; watching the cash whizzing along the overhead wires to the cashiers' booth was a real treat. Everything was different in those days. I can't remember many of the names of the staff who worked in the main store, strange really, because they were all so friendly and would always have a friendly word to say when you went by.

When I think of the Co-op now, I immediately think of the comedy programme, *Are You Being Served.* So much of it is reminiscent of those days. Even the characters remind me of certain people, but I won't go down that pathway.

They were happy days, more innocent certainly and you weren't scared to walk down the road on your own after dark or even in the daylight. I can remember walking down the road of an evening to meet John coming home from the afternoon shift. The thought never entered my head to be scared or that the flat could be burgled. How times change, and now everyone locks their doors and ensures that their property is secure.

After our honeymoon, I had never been so happy; I had a wonderful husband, a good job. John's family and mine were really supportive of us, and a lot to look forward to. Neither of us were particularly ambitious; we wanted to own a house and then have a couple of children. I wanted a girl first and then a boy, but that was in the distant future because we both knew we had to get some money behind us first before we moved up the housing ladder.

John and I still worked for TASCOS. At one time, married couples couldn't work in the company, but fortunately for us they had relaxed the rules by that time.

Sid Watts again offered me the use of his caravan saying we could use it whenever we had a free weekend. He rarely found time to go as he had a very full diary of civic and charitable engagements, so we took him up on his kind offer and made our way to Wales as often as we could. John had a car so we avoided the use of public transport, thank goodness!

A few months after having lived in the upstairs rooms of Grandma Arnall's house, we were offered a flat to rent. We were delighted. It was a company flat so it was tied property but we weren't overly bothered by that, as should I leave, John would still be working for the Transport Department, or vice versa.

We went to view it; the flat was in Kings Heath above the grocery shop on the High Street. The flat entrance was in Bank Street. It had steps leading up to a gate then there was a small yard and facing were two doors; our flat was to be 64b. Compared to where we were living, it was huge. I fell in love with it immediately and couldn't wait to accept the offer.

On entering the flat, you were in a very small basic kitchen that led into a very long hall, the bathroom was on the right then just beyond that there was a wide opening with a window, next to that on the right was quite a large room that could be used as a bedroom or dining room, next came the stairs that led up to a large bedroom to the left that looked over the High Street, and on the right was a very small bedroom with no window.

At the end of the hall was a very large lounge that was heated by a Parkray fire.

To my eyes, the flat was a dream come true and we moved in the following week. We had to furnish it as we went along. Nevertheless, the joy of having a bathroom and hot running water was sheer unadulterated luxury.

Our next-door neighbour, Mr Tabberner, worked as a coalman for the Co-op. He had a son, Christopher, who was around ten years of age at the time we moved in. I don't know what happened to his wife, but they were very good neighbours. Mr Tabberner was quite a bit older than we were and kept himself to himself; they were nice people.

Not long after moving into Bank Street, I discovered I was pregnant. That changed our life plan, but we were not unduly worried. It would just take a bit longer to save for our house. We were quite excited and I hoped that we would have a daughter, but should the baby be a boy, that would be fine by us.

I signed up with John's family doctor, Dr Hodgeson, who lived not far from our flat along the High Street. John and his parents said he was extremely nice.

The first time I visited his surgery there were some beautiful bowls of sweet smelling hyacinths on the table in his very cold waiting room! Despite his advice, I was against going into hospital for our baby and booked in with a lovely midwife to have a home birth. We were excited and looking forward to the birth in mid-July, wondering if the baby would arrive on my birthday the 16th.

I carried on working and made arrangements to return to my job after the birth because we were both determined to buy our own house. We loved our flat, but realised it presented problems for the future with the steps leading up to it. There was no way round it; I would have to take the pram downstairs first then go back for the baby and bag etc. Then I would have to do the whole process in reverse on returning from shopping or visiting.

It was great living above the grocery shop as I was allowed to use the back entrance to the shop once they got to know me. So handy; if I forgot anything, I would just pop downstairs, go in the back door of the shop and get whatever we needed.

It was great as well; living on the High Street was smashing for getting shopping in, and catching a bus into Birmingham was brilliant.

I got to know the shop assistants and a couple of them became friends, Josie and Ruth. They would come up and have a coffee from time to time. Once I left work, I saw more of our friends Hazel and Les, who by this time had a son named Christopher. I would sometimes get John to drop me off at their house in Small Heath.

A few weeks before the birth, we decided we would take a week's holiday and booked up at a Boatel in Dartmouth. There were fantastic views of the water from the lounge and we spent many hours looking out. I missed our walks, but with the birth not to far off, the time I would have spent walking was now taken up by sleeping in the afternoons. John would take himself off for a walk while I was resting. All too soon, it was time to return home ready for the birth of our first child, in those days you had no idea what sex your baby would be. Of course, we didn't mind whether we had a boy or a girl, but secretly I hoped for a daughter to be our firstborn, as I had never forgotten how much I loved my sister Jane.

Mid 1960s

We had a couple of friends, Pat and Ray, in for tea and supper on the 11th July 1965. I had seen the midwife earlier that week and everything was okay despite my being nearly a week overdue. I was quite blasé about it all and sat drinking a rum and coke and eating pickled onions. Both were my cravings during the latter half of my pregnancy. Not being a drinker, craving rum was unbelievable! Ray was an ambulance driver. Pat looked at me around 10.30 p.m. and said, 'I think you'll go into labour tonight, Carol, your face looks a bit swollen.'

That made me think, 'No not more weight, please.' I'd already put on over three stones in weight and felt a bit like the Michelin X Man. Pat and Ray went shortly afterwards and we retired to bed.

I woke about 1.45 a.m. feeling a little uncomfortable and John phoned for the midwife, who arrived quite quickly. We had put a single bed in the small room downstairs and she got us organised; hot water, plenty of towels, and the inevitable cups of tea. I was a little disappointed to find that the midwife who had looked after me throughout the pregnancy was on holiday in Austria, but nevertheless, the young lady who was with me was very nice. If I remember correctly, she described her position as a pupil midwife.

That first hour passed very swiftly and she had settled me into bed and then took her knitting out, telling us that I had quite a few hours to go. The thought went through my head that no way was I standing this pain any longer and I told her I was going to push. Her knitting went straight up in the air and she almost screamed, 'No, no, you can't.'

My reply was, 'Yes, I can and I am.' I did and our daughter Helen arrived shortly after 3 a.m. on the 12th July 1965.

I don't remember much more after that as apparently I lost a lot of blood and became delirious.

The doctor was sent for and also John's mom arrived. I didn't get to hold our much-wanted daughter until late into the next day, and was so disappointed in myself. I thought I had missed out on a magic moment and always regretted not having held her as soon as she was born.

I was supposed to stay in bed for a couple of weeks, but I was out of bed a few days after the birth; I couldn't bear the thought of lying around any longer. Apparently, it hadn't been so long ago that women were expected to 'lie in' for six weeks, so I suppose two weeks was quite an improvement, though still too long for me.

I did feel quite weak and tearful for a while afterwards, but John's mom was very good and helped us a lot. John naturally had to return to work to keep the money coming in. Men weren't encouraged to take part in the birth of a child then, but I was so glad he stuck around when Helen was born. Things might not have run so smoothly otherwise.

I remember I was feeding Helen in the kitchen when she was a couple of weeks old when I heard a knock on the door; on opening it, I was greeted by a man. He introduced himself as someone from the school authority and wanted details of Helen for when she started school. I thought there's nothing like getting them young.

One day while still on maternity leave, I popped into the local church and asked the vicar if I could help anyone in the community for a couple of hours or so during the weekdays. He asked if I attended church on a Sunday morning. I explained that I had a small baby – pretty obvious really as she was in her pram with me – and my parents-in-law went to church so I didn't have a babysitter, and also that John worked Sundays. He replied that, when I attended church regularly, then he would find me something to do. I was so hurt I vowed never to set foot in that church again.

My mom-in-law would pop round and if necessary, she would take Helen off for a few hours and bless her heart, she even looked after her for a good while when I returned to work, she was golden to us, always has been.

Eventually I found a child-minder who lived not far from the office so I could drop Helen off on my way to work and collect her on my return. Unfortunately, she didn't settle and I found another woman willing to take her. I promised myself though if our baby didn't settle, then I would finish work.

The woman I found lived about seven minutes walk from our flat. Her name was Floss Brookes. What a find she was, a truly wonderful woman.

Floss was the female equivalent of the Pied Piper. Kids gravitated to her like bees to a jar of honey. They adored her and likewise, she adored them.

Nothing was too much trouble for Floss; anything to do with kids was okay by her. I really enjoyed her company and on my Wednesday afternoons off, we would walk down to the local park with the children and sit on a bench while the little ones had the time of their lives in the park. We had many a good chat together in the park, usually about men I might add.

Even later on when we moved to Staffordshire, Floss would visit us and she was always more than welcome. She had three children if I remember correctly, they were Diane and David, who were heading for their teens when I first knew them, and then there was Jeannie, who was a delightful youngster of about five years of age. John, Floss' husband, worked at a glass company called Triplex, I think it was in Kings Norton. The Brookes were a lovely family and as with all lost friends, you wonder what happened to them as the years pass by.

As you get older, time has a habit of passing very, very quickly; it seems as if you blink your eyes and twenty years have passed, blink them again and thirty have gone. Hmm, you don't really want to blink again after that.

After a while, I felt like a change of work and applied for a job that was vacant at the Kings Heath store in the club repayment office. This office was at the rear of the shop and was run by a woman named Irene. My application was successful and once settled in, I really enjoyed the work. One of the reasons was I didn't have the mile or so to walk to Stirchley every day; the office was only a short walk from our flat. So overall, I thought I had made a good move. Everything about the job itself was enjoyable, even the figure work, which I had tried to avoid for so long. Customers were popping down to the office all day making their repayments and sometimes applying for another loan. If successful, they would pick it up the following week. It felt quite strange at first to think that now I was passing on the customer check to someone who was doing my old job. One of the women who worked with me for a short while in the club repayment office was Mrs Reed. She was a very pleasant person to work with; she was in her fifties at that time, but had a youthful outlook on everything despite knowing a great sadness in her early-married life.

What happened was her son developed Scarlet Fever when he was about seven years of age and unfortunately, the severity of the attack killed him. Of course, poor Mrs Reed was devastated and said that a few months after the little boy's death, she was looking out of his bedroom window, the sun was shining and children were playing in the street, women were chatting over their garden fences, and she realised that life went on regardless of what happens to you and yours.

In addition, a woman named Irene worked in the office with me, I can't remember her surname, but she would come out with some strange sayings. Such as, 'Night night, sleep tight, don't let the bed bugs bite!'

Irene was a widow; she lived in quite a large house in King's Heath and took in lodgers to help eke out her money.

Another even stranger saying was when she saw a pregnant woman, 'There she goes, on her toes, going to have a baby, I suppose.' I don't know where she got her sayings from. Irene was a lovely woman to work with and we got on like a house on fire. There were plenty of laughs, usually at our boss's expense, but it was always good-natured.

The boss of the shop was Mr Lloyd. He was a tall man with a rather loud voice, funny how you remember things about people. He was always smartly dressed, as was everyone else for that matter. Ladies didn't wear trousers for work in those days. It seemed to be an unwritten rule that we wore smart suits or skirt and a white blouse. The men were expected to wear a suit, shirt, and tie. For myself, I have always preferred to dress casually and on arriving home from work, I would always change as soon as possible. It's different nowadays employers' are much more relaxed in their attitude to what their employees' wear.

A Mrs Davies would drop into the office from time to time to audit the books. She was a small lady who wore extremely dark-rimmed glasses and kept her hair scraped back in a tight bun at the back of her neck, she was always very neatly dressed and I noticed she never wore any other footwear than black lace-up shoes. Funny what you remember about people. You felt guilty the minute you saw her marching towards the office with her briefcase, she was very strict and your heart was always in your mouth in case she found any discrepancies. Fortunately for me, there was only one occasion that this happened.

I was cashing up one day on the desk area at the back of the office out of sight of the front counter. Mrs Davies arrived and I shot down the office to open the door for her, I placed the account book on the desk, Mrs Davies discovered to my horror that the book was five pounds down. Horrors, that was a lot of money in those days and I showed her my purse, handbag, even my coat pockets, and she searched them! The fiver was discovered as she closed the book, she had unintentionally placed it on top of the five-pound note that I hadn't returned to the cash box when I rushed to let her in; my fault for being over-keen to open the door. I felt guilty about that happening for months afterwards.

Bryntegan and Wales

John's parents owned a cottage just over the Herefordshire border. It was called Bryntegan.

The first time I saw it, I thought how lovely it was, a real old-fashioned whitewashed country cottage. Bryntegan was right on the edge of the moors. Access to the moorland entailed a very steep climb up the hill behind the cottage, but it was well worth it as the views were wonderful. We would go down occasionally for a visit and it was an enjoyable day out. There was a farm just along the lane; in later years I found out it was once The Sun Inn, Mom-in-law once actually dug up an old beer mug in the cottage garden! There also a small church with a delightful churchyard just along from the farm. Occasionally, the horse or sheep from the farm were put in the churchyard to keep the grass down. Over the years, we made many trips to Bryntegan and as the pace of life increased, times got noisier and noisier, so it was a small oasis of calm that we looked forward to visiting.

We also carried on visiting Sid Watt's caravan some weekends and for our summer holidays. We would stand on the beach and on hot sunny days we would watch the dolphins leaping and playing far out to sea. It was a wonderful place for a holiday.

One year we went to the caravan and our daughter developed a bad stomach infection. We visited the local doctor, who was very nice and attentive, and I asked him if it would be advisable to cut the holiday short. He said there was no need to spoil our break and to carry on with the holiday. I thought of his words often when I was in the toilet block washing the nappies out for the remainder of the week. I wondered if he was having a joke about spoiling the hols or not. The most important thing though was the baby quickly made a full recovery after we arrived home.

One incident has stuck in my mind over the years. The shop on the caravan site used to sell novels and I began to notice quite a few of the ones I bought had already been read. Some of the pages would be grubby and look used. I was paying full price for them and felt a bit miffed about it. I mentioned this to Sid Watts when we were chatting about the holiday and he was quite taken aback. He must have said something to the person who ran the shop as ever afterwards, the books were in mint condition.

Around that time, we decided it would be nice to leave the city life behind and thought we might re-locate to Llandrindod Wells. This was not far from Brookside, where we had spent our honeymoon, and we loved the area. In fact, we had spent a couple of long weekends there with our friends Diane from TASCOS and Robert, who she had married. We both applied for jobs at the garage in Llandrindod; John for a mechanic's job and I applied for a secretarial position. We were both offered the jobs and then went flat hunting. Eventually, we found one to our liking and took it on. We went one weekend with a couple of friends and took a few miscellaneous items with us. As we entered the front door and were walking down the hall, a quite elderly couple approached us, and looking us up and down, obviously not impressed by our casual clothes, they told us that we had to use the back door. Of course, we complied; like heck we did. I thought what a nice welcoming couple they were and felt slighted. After showing our friends around our new home-to-be, we left via the way we came through the front door.

Our plans were progressing well and despite the unpleasantness at the flat, we were still looking forward to our new home and jobs.

I had been feeling a little off colour for a few weeks and put it down to the general rushing about due to the move. Then I sat down one night and realised that the son we so desperately wanted to complete our family was on his way; well, I hoped it was a boy. This was a complete surprise and after careful thought, we decided not to move. I didn't fancy being so far away from friends and family with a new baby. In addition, it was only a two-bedroom flat. Plans in disarray, we knew we had some serious decisions to make. Finally, we cancelled our new jobs and the flat.

On Saturdays we often went into Birmingham to have a look round. One such Saturday we were in the city when a sign for a Psychic Fair caught my eye. The Fair was being held that weekend in the Bingley Hall. For some inexplicable reason, I felt drawn towards it. We had our daughter in her pushchair so we left the shopping centre and made our way up to the hall. I would like to say that I had a reading and afterwards everything became clearer to me, and that we were going to win the football pools and become instant millionaires. (There was no Lotto in those days.) Truth to tell, apart from the people reading cards and palms and runes, all the usual stuff, John and I with Helen in her pushchair felt very conspicuous, as we were the only people in the Hall. Why I remember it so vividly is because I remembered how when I was quite young I was walking to school one day when we lived in Northfield and I saw a ghost. It was nothing very exciting or earth shattering; I was walking up St. Helier's Road in Northfield. The road ahead was deserted when all of a sudden a young girl appeared as if from nowhere not far in front of me. I squinted my eyes to see if I could recognise her, but I didn't. She wasn't far away and I would say she was about nine or ten years of age. I tried to catch her up, but as I drew a little nearer to her, she disappeared in front of my eyes. I blinked and blinked again no young girl, in fact, no one at all in sight, in front or when I looked behind me. To say I was puzzled was an understatement and I continued my walk to school thinking that perhaps I had imagined seeing the girl. However, I had definitely seen her and decided I had seen a ghost. I knew better than to tell anyone at school or at home. I just knew that would be good ammunition to throw at me by the boys and schoolchildren. For once, I kept my mouth shut.

The memory of the girl ghost stuck in my memory and whenever I read a paper or magazine containing a ghost story, I was compelled to read it first. I still do.

Never did I imagine that day that in years to come, I would become so fascinated by the paranormal that I would become a tarot reader myself and write books of ghost stories. Indeed, if anyone had told me then that this would happen, I am certain I wouldn't have believed it.

Late 1960s

As my pregnancy progressed and the move that never happened was sorted, we knew there was no way we could continue living in our flat. Only being two bedrooms was definitely a negative and having two small children and a pram to drag up and down the steps was the deciding factor that we would have to find a new home.

One evening I noticed an advertisement in the Evening Mail. It was an advertisement for new houses being built on the Five Oaks Estate at a place called Brereton in Staffordshire. They were asking for fifty pounds deposit to secure a new three-bedroom, semi-detached house. Fifty pounds was a lot of money in the 1960s, of course, but we discussed it and decided to go and take a look that coming weekend.

We fell in love with the place; Brereton was a small country village on the edge of Cannock Chase, the house and the surrounding area ticked all the right boxes for us, and we applied for one of them. To our delight, our application was accepted; a house and garden was something to really look forward to. True, we would be quite a distance from our families, but not as far as Wales, and the big pull was the house and the garden.

Pauline, meanwhile, had bought a bungalow in Tamworth so she wasn't going to be very far away from us once we moved so that was a huge plus.

I didn't gain much weight at all with my second pregnancy and despite the doctor's advice, I chose to have the baby at home again. Hospitals held no appeal at all for me. I did go to the local maternity home The Sorrento for a few tests and wasn't impressed by it. I settled for a home delivery.

Ten days before my due date, the midwife visited me and pronounced all was well. Again, I had cravings for pickled onions and always had a jar to hand, but not rum this time, thank goodness. The following morning at about eight fifteen, I woke with a niggling stomach ache, so John took our daughter round to Vicarage Road, where his parents lived, as Mom had said she would look after her at a minute's notice should we feel the need. I decided to have a bath to settle my stomach down, but if anything it made it worse and I thought, 'I had better get upstairs fast.' As I stumbled up the hall, John came back saying that he thought he was needed. Too right he was, I only just made it onto the bed when the baby made a very fast entrance. Poor John didn't know what to do. He said, 'Oh, it's a boy and he looks like he needs a wash. Shall I wrap him in this newspaper?'

Men, I thought, and then I heard the midwife calling out, 'Oh, my God the baby has arrived.' John had been so concerned that he had phoned for the midwife from his mom's. She tore up the stairs and took immediate charge; John went out and about telling the neighbours we now had a son. Many of them were amazed as they hadn't even realised I was pregnant. I was though and how; Paul weighed eight and a half pounds, just over two whole pounds more than Helen did. The midwife cleaned everything up and John returned to say he was off to work! Then the midwife took her leave.

So there I was, lying in bed in considerable discomfort and our new son in his carrycot fast asleep. I think I drifted off for a while then woke feeling very uncomfortable indeed. I didn't know what to do, the telephone was downstairs in the lounge and there was no one who I could call on for help. My head felt muzzy and as I began to drift away again, I realised I was bleeding heavily. The next thing I remembered was hearing the midwife's voice saying,

'Come on, girl, come on,' as she kneaded my stomach to try to stem the blood flow. Afterwards, she said she had been on the point of phoning for an ambulance. She also said she just felt an urge to come and check on me as she was worried. Thank goodness she did or I might not be here writing this story.

The next day I got up and was ready to carry on with my life, that is until the midwife arrived. 'Back to bed,' she boomed.

'No way,' I said; I would just have a rest for a couple of hours. I wanted to take charge of my small family now. She had other ideas. I wanted to start going out after a few days, but I couldn't as Paul developed a snuffly cold and he was confined indoors as well.

Fortunately, he was a very good baby and we were soon out and about. Helen hadn't slept through the night once for the first eighteen months and when I was carrying Paul, I had many misgivings thinking of the sleep deprivation to come. We were lucky because he slept through from the start and was a contented baby; he always had a beaming smile for everyone who peeped into his pram and cooed at him.

Not long before we left the High Street flat, I was looking out of the lounge window and was astonished to see thieves robbing the shoe shop across the road. What was astonishing about it was everywhere was well lit up as it was around ten in the evening, and the road was as busy as ever with people everywhere. We called the police; the police station was just down the road so the officers were soon on the scene and arrested the men. I thought we might have been called as witnesses, but no one came to take a statement and I presumed there was no need for our evidence as it was such a straightforward case.

Our house transaction went smoothly and when Paul was a few months old, we moved to Staffordshire. John borrowed a lorry from my father's workplace and we were on the way with the help of one of his friends.

A new house meant a lot of hard work scrubbing the floors to rid them of cement, etc. The garden was a tip. The workers had dumped ours and everyone else's rubbish onto our back garden. It was a terrible mess inside and out and I just didn't know where to start. It was a very wide and long garden, so I wasn't looking forward to clearing it.

John had found a mechanic's job at a garage going by the name of Three Spires in Lichfield, so wages were assured for the immediate future. Because I felt so lonely and isolated, to start with he came home at lunchtime to make sure we were all okay.

It was a huge change for me. Having been used to crowds of people and constant traffic, Brereton felt like we had landed on a different planet. In addition, I didn't know a soul. Talk about depressed. I wanted to go home on the second day. I really thought I had made a dreadful mistake. Everywhere was so quiet. You could even hear birds singing outside. It might have been easier for me if we had had the telephone installed, but that required quite a wait; and when it was first installed we were on a party line. In the end, I rolled my sleeves up and got on with the job of cleaning the house and clearing the garden thoroughly; vowing to return to Birmingham at the first opportunity.

Fortunately, my circle of acquaintances grew and a routine became established.

Helen started at George Vickers Infants School along the A51 not far from the local library. That suited me down to the ground as I missed Kings Heath library and I would pop in as often as possible when I collected her from school. George Vickers belonged to Hob Hill Junior School, which was along Armitage Lane. Being small, George Vickers had a wonderful atmosphere and you could tell as you went through the entrance door how

86

happy the children were. I had no qualms about leaving Helen; I knew she would settle down, make friends, and was pleased that she did.

Three times a week, a group of us young women would walk down 'town' to do our shopping. We all had babies in prams with carrying trays underneath where we could put our shopping. When we reached The Horsefair, we stopped off at the local café to have coffee and sausage rolls. We would sit at the breakfast bar on the stools watching the traffic pass by on the busy A51. Once refreshed, we would get our goods and then walk home.

At that time, there were two wallpaper shops in the town and I remember once buying a large tin of paint from one of the shops, only to have the lid shoot off and orange paint go all over my red trouser suit and the pavement, horrors, what a mess to try to clean up; I was so embarrassed. I later found out that I could have returned the tin and they would have replaced it with a new one; instead, I let John pop down at the weekend to buy another one.

1970s

John found himself a new job at Bradbury and Browns Garage in Armitage Road not far from home. He was a mechanic in the workshop. He no longer came home for lunch and life seemed quite settled for a while. I quietly still vowed to go home to Birmingham, but with property prices slowly creeping up, this was becoming a distant dream along with winning the football pools.

We still visited our parents when we could. This was reserved for weekends and when we had saved enough for petrol money. I saw Pauline more than anyone else and we were always on the phone chatting together. I was shocked when she told me one day that she was divorcing Peter, and as if that wasn't bad enough, she was moving back to Birmingham. Pauline had found work at Dunlop so it made sense that she should find a place nearer to her job.

I decided to find work and visited an employment agency in Rugeley, who found me a job at a factory called Thorn Automation on the main Brereton Road situated between Rugeley and Brereton, virtually on the borders.

If someone had told me then that a few years down the line, I would be writing about the ghost who haunted the old house in the grounds, again I wouldn't have believed them.

My job was as a PA to a man who in turn was in charge of the department; I cannot remember what the department's function was. I was thrilled and looked forward to the challenge, albeit nervously.

The first few days passed quite quickly, but I had an underlying feeling that my face didn't fit. For some reason or other, it got so bad that when I was in the office, a deathly silence began to reign. I was a lot younger than most of the staff so I was quite disturbed by this atmosphere.

Whether it was the stress or what I don't know, but I developed a bad back and found sitting or even walking decidedly painful. To add to my troubles, I was called into the boss' office and found to my surprise the personnel manager was standing beside him. My heart quailed and I felt quite frightened when I looked at their faces, they were so stern and intimidating.

I had taken my shorthand notebook and pencil in with me and owing to feeling under the weather, I nervously dropped them. Because of being in terrible pain, I struggled to pick them up and neither of those big brave men offered to assist me. They kept me standing and due to my muddled thoughts, I found it difficult to grasp what they were rattling on about. After being told to return to the office, I was greeted again by the deathly silence and I began to realise that I had been given an official warning. I was devastated; this had never happened to me before and when I told John that evening, he was quite shocked and remarked how cruel they were to treat me like that, apart from which it was obvious I was in a great deal of pain.

The next day, I signed off work ill, which I was, and they had made me feel worse. Normally I would work myself into the ground no matter how ill I felt, but I decided that I owed them no loyalty, and eventually after a couple of months allowing myself to recover fully, I sent in my notice. I certainly didn't want to work for a boss who lacked the basic human instinct of kindness.

To this day, I don't know why I was treated so abominably.

I soon found another job at a photograph laboratory in Redbrook Lane called Colourtrend. I loved it. I worked in the Quality Control Department and my job involved altering the colour strengths on the photographs that were wrong. I really felt as if I had fallen on my feet. I liked the staff and the open plan work scene where you walked from one department to the next. The laboratory had not long been open and it was a tremendous success.

Unfortunately, due to the nature of the work, I was again sitting for long periods on a high stool with next to no back support. My back problem returned with a vengeance. The team leader, whose name I think was Derek, did everything he could to help, bringing me cushions and even allowing me breaks to walk around.

I went to see a consultant at Stafford Hospital, which has now been moved to the outskirts of Stafford, making it even more difficult to attend as two buses are now involved getting to it from Rugeley. I was allowed time out to attend physiotherapy three times a week. I was so disappointed when I eventually realised that I would have to leave my job. The company were very good and told me that if my circumstances changed, there would always be a job for me. What a difference to Thorn Automation, who couldn't wait to get me out. I was devastated at leaving the laboratory, but for very different reasons this time.

After a time when I had recovered my health again, I decided to find work that involved me moving around and had a complete change of direction. I went to work at Bradbury and Brown Garage, where my husband worked. My job was to clean the cars in the showroom. Strangely enough, even though it was a completely new work experience, I quite enjoyed it. My colleagues were all very nice and we quickly became friends. There was many a laugh and joke amongst us, the mechanics, and the men in the spray shop. I quickly settled in.

Cyril, a retired man, worked part-time driving for the showroom and Yvonne, who worked with me as a car cleaner, would go out together when a car needed to be collected. Another lady also worked as a driver, her name was Kath. When she wasn't around then Cyril and Yvonne swung into action. I became fast friends with Cyril and got to know his wife, Doris, very well. Our two families often got together at weekends and when we visited them, we were always made more than welcome. They had a wonderful bungalow at Hill Ridware. I can still see Doris and me swinging on the hammock in their garden on a warm summer's evening. They loved our children and always made a huge fuss of them.

Doris was a wonderful tailor. Cyril regularly took her to Fleetwood, not far from Blackpool, to get her materials. Apparently, there was a very good market there and it made a good day out for the couple.

For a short time before going to Bradbury and Brown, I had worked in the showrooms at the Imperial Garage along the Armitage Road just around the corner from Thomson Road. Again, I would have been amazed if someone told me I would be writing about a ghost that appeared from time to time in the vicinity of the garage. For a while, I worked in the car showrooms alongside a mother and daughter cleaning the cars. I then moved out onto the forecourt serving petrol with another employee, who everyone called Old Tom. He was quite elderly and we got on like a house on fire. There was also another man named Ken, who worked the opposite shift to Tom. I worked the late shift sometimes finishing around midnight. I would walk up Thomson Road in the early hours with the day's takings in my bag. I cannot ever remember feeling scared or worried about this, but I don't think I would be so happy to do it nowadays.

There were plenty of police patrols along the Armitage Road and they would often pull onto the forecourt and check that I was okay.

Decimalisation came into being while I worked at the Imperial, and from what I can remember I only made one mistake giving out change so for someone who was dumb at maths, I was learning fast. I enjoyed my time at the garage, but decided to move to Bradbury and Brown after a while.

One incident that happened when I worked at Bradbury and Brown has stuck in my memory and I will never forget it. I had never taken any driving lessons, but a car needed moving urgently so one of the showroom staff urged me to move it, saying they would guide me. Big mistake, while watching them a car parked behind me and I never saw it. I thought as I heard the smash, there goes another job. However, to my relief, Gerald Brown the owner took it quite well and I promised never to drive unsupervised again until I had passed my test.

Another incident nearly finished me off, it was my job to make the tea from time to time; the kettle we used was in a bay adjoining the office where we worked. I popped into the bay one morning, plugged the kettle in, and then switched it on; I found myself flung right across the bay. What a shock that was in more ways than one. Hasty repairs were quickly carried out and thank goodness nothing like that happened again.

When I first started at Bradbury and Brown, Kenny Whitehouse was the service manager and when he left, Richard Mason took over.

The company remained trading for a number of years and I was quite shocked to hear a few years ago that the owner Gerald Brown had died.

The garage is now derelict, Gerald Brown's daughter took the business over when he died, but unfortunately it closed suddenly and the place is now in a dreadful state.

Prices were rising rapidly and we longed for a detached house. John took on a part-time driving job at a bakery in Wharf Road. One day he casually mentioned that the job of tea lady was vacant. Of course, I decided to apply. The hours suited me and the pay was more than I was receiving. Arriving for the appointment, my heart sank at seeing a long line of applicants for the job. I really thought I didn't stand a chance. I walked into the boss' office and was surprised to see it was a lady doing the interview, as John had told me a Mr Graham Hindley would be doing them. Nevertheless, I had a little chat with the lady; I later learnt her name was Mrs Chiltern. At the end of the interview, she shocked me when she offered me the job. Apparently, Mr Graham had told her that if she thought I was suitable, then she could offer me the job.

I think I got the job on the back of John being such a reliable part-time worker.

I started the following week after giving my notice in at Bradbury and Brown.

I enjoyed working at Hindley's Bakery and quickly settled down. The staff was very nice, and once I had learnt whose cup was whose, I was fine. I never thought I would remember putting a face to a cup and who had sugar and who preferred their tea or coffee black, but eventually it worked out.

One unfortunate incident happened when I forgot to switch the water heater on one morning and realised almost too late that I wouldn't be able to make the tea in time for the first break. I could see the sack looming on the horizon again. I managed though and calm soon returned.

Everyone apart from the office staff used the canteen throughout the day. There were people coming and going all day long.

I remember the bakery strike very well, and how hard the staff worked, sometimes through the night to provide extra bread for the Cannock Chase area. I went back of an evening for a couple of hours to make tea and tidy up for the workers. Everyone pulled together to get through the strike.

At times groups of schoolchildren would be shown around the bakery and I would serve up glasses of orange juice and a tray of cakes for them. The bakery staff also had a tray of cakes provided for them at break-time. When it was very hot in the summer, Mr Graham sent out for ice-cream and ice-lollies for the staff as temperatures could become unbearable.

It was quite a walk to the bakery in the mornings and back in the afternoons, so I started to take driving lessons with Horace Copes Driving School. He employed a driver called Richard Wood, who we got to know socially as well. He got me through my second driving test much to my relief; this was in the hot summer of 1976.

A new world opened up once I could drive. I had a Morris Traveller and getting to work and back became a joy. Shopping was no longer a chore and I soon spread my wings, enjoying my independence.

Up until that time, work had been very easy to get.

In between all my jobs, I had worked as a cleaner at Spode House in Brereton. This was a lovely place to work; as you entered the building you were greeted with a beautiful warm atmosphere. I remember sitting with all the other employees at the huge table in the kitchen having our breaks. The priest sat at the head of the table, and one day a bee settled on his hand and he spoke to it. If that had happened to me, you wouldn't have seen me for dust.

What a gracious building it was, lots of corridors below stairs, with small rooms leading off. Someone said that these had at one time been the monks' cells. At the time I worked there, Spode was used as a conference centre and I got to know one of the nuns staying there. She was in the order of The Poor Clare's based at Lynmouth. She wrote to me for many years and then her letters suddenly stopped. I did write to the Mother Superior asking what had happened to her, but never received a reply.

Whilst at Spode, I met Diane a very pretty novice. She had the most wonderful long dark hair. I was astonished when she told me that she would lose it all when she was accepted into the Order. I don't know whether she finally took her vows as we lost touch.

In later years, I was to write about a ghostly happening in the grounds of Spode.

I regret now not taking more notes of some of the old houses I worked at, but then when you are young and trying to earn a living and busy bringing up a family, you really don't have that much time to notice your surroundings. You just get on with your job.

That job came to an end and in between whiles, I worked at a company called Ketch Plastics in Lichfield in their Quality Control Department.

I also worked for a time at Longdon Hall School in Longdon. Unfortunately, my back trouble returned with a vengeance so that job, like many of my other jobs, didn't last very long.

I retained my interest in the paranormal, and around this time, I decided to try the Ouija Board. I wasn't put off by all the stories that they were nasty evil things that attracted bad spirits. Along with a few friends, we set it up one night and were astounded when the pointer moved on its own accord and began spelling out messages. 'Who's pushing it?' someone asked. Immediately the people using it quickly made denials and a ghostly silence descended on the room as the pointer moved faster and faster around the board. It gave out many messages that no one could possibly have known about, and we were all astounded by this mysterious piece of equipment. We wondered how a small plastic pointer could seemingly move on its own volition and point to the letters of the alphabet and numbers printed in a semi-circle around the board spelling out messages. After each message, the room temperature seemed to drop, making the whole affair seem even spookier. The messages carried on coming thick and fast for quite a while, but then their tone seemed to change in content and instead of giving out positive answers to questions, negative ones began to be spelt through and the atmosphere became charged. We all became very worried and packed it away. In fact, I refused to have it in the house and it was thrown in the shed; when we moved, it went into the dustbin.

Over the years, I have realised that really the board was not a scary object; we simply frightened each other. At the end of the day, it was just a printed card with letters and numbers on it!

A few of us ladies would go round to the local church hall on a Saturday night to play bingo. It was a chance to meet up and have a chat. At that time, there were no huge Bingo Halls anywhere, just a few local ones. This particular one was very basic; the bingo balls were pulled from a hat and quite a few times the wrong number was called, but it was all very light-hearted and enjoyable. I remember we had to wait for the butcher, who was always late, and we never ever started without him. I think the highest prize then was about five shillings, which is 25 pence in new money. Hardly a fortune, but no one went expecting to win a huge amount.

Our cat was pure white hence the name Snowy, not very original I know! Now this cat, like all cats, had a mind of its own and it went anywhere and everywhere it wanted to; unlike most cats it decided for the first few years that it would use the house as its toilet, despite a cat tray in every room.

We had visitors one day and I was boiling some milk on the electric cooker when the most awful smell rent the air. I thought, 'Oh, the milk is off,' but I noticed to my horror the cat had peed on the cooker. I was horrified and didn't know what to say; the guests left shortly afterwards.

Another time, Snowy went missing and after many searches over three days, I had almost decided that she had gone for good, when I thought I heard a meow in one of the bedrooms. I checked all three rooms, but no sign of Snowy. Then I heard her again and on opening what I thought was an empty wardrobe, out stalked Snowy, tail in the air as if to say, 'What did you do that for?' I haven't a clue how she came to be locked inside the wardrobe, but I will never forget it.

Another time I was chatting to some neighbours on the pavement outside our house when one of them said, 'Look at your cat, Carol.' I glanced back at the house and was shocked to see Snowy perched on the bedroom window ledge from where she proceeded not to jump, but to walk down the front of the house until she almost reached ground level, where she jumped, shook herself, stuck her tail in the air and went walkabout. We had stood with our mouths wide open watching this scene in amazement, and from then on, Snowy was famous as the 'cat walker'.

She certainly led a charmed life, and moved with us to the Brereton Road and from there to Leathermill Lane, where she lived to the ripe old age of eighteen before she sadly died. Even at Leathermill Lane, she left her mark on my favourite sheepskin rug as if to say, 'I'm still in charge.'

I have never really recovered from the episode of the cat having kittens in our bed when we were children. The cats we acquired were really for the children, but it fell to me or John to look after them, of course.

Tessa our dog was a wild character for such a small mongrel; she was a collie-cross, black and white marking with a permanent grin on her face.

Tessa loathed the dog that lived in a house across the road. This dog was called Sally, and from the word go they loathed the sight of each other.

One day someone came to the front door, and as I opened it a small black and white tornado rushed past me, I screamed and before I knew it, there was a screech of brakes and poor little Tessa had been hit. She had seen Sally from our front window, seized her opportunity, and dashed out. I was so upset and thought she had been killed, but no. She was obviously very shocked, but we got her to the vets and her only injury was to her tail; the damage to it resulted in her losing her wag, lucky Tessa. The car driver returned the next day to see how she was and was very relieved to hear she was fine.

The dog she hated, Sally, had a habit of trapping people in the telephone box that stood near her home. There was one lady in particular she took a dislike to; the lady in question would visit the telephone box most days to call her fiancée, remember, there were no mobile phones in those days, in fact when we first moved to Brereton, we were on a party line. Sally would keep circling the phone box the whole time the lady was in it. By the time she had finished her call, Sally had worked herself up into a real frenzy and the poor woman would be calling for help so she could get away from the telephone box. I often wondered why she didn't go to the call box along the main road where she would have been far safer.

Tessa lived for many years and came with us when we eventually moved to Leathermill Lane; unfortunately, she escaped from the back garden not long after we moved. Poor little thing got run over not far from our house in Brereton Road. I felt incredibly sad about this, as she was such a little survivor; to think we kept her safely while living on a main road for so long and then she lost her life returning to our old house. She had gone deaf and no doubt this attributed to her death as she wouldn't have heard the car, but of course, I was to blame for not ensuring the fencing was A1 before letting her out to play. I have carried the guilt ever since.

The first dog we ever had we had to give away; we had her when I was expecting Helen and as soon as the baby arrived, the dog turned vicious with jealousy and I couldn't trust her in the house. Unfortunately she had to go because she tried to attack the baby twice.

The years quickly passed and eventually John went to work at Lea Hall Colliery. I hated the thought of him working underground, but he wanted to and having such a good wage coming in enabled us to buy a detached Victorian house along the Brereton Road not far from Rugeley Town Centre.

We were able to do this very quickly as we sold our house in Lodge Road immediately to a friend of mine. In fact, my friend was so determined to have it that she took out a bridging loan to secure the sale, and sent me a letter to Butlin's Holiday Camp in Minehead where we were on holiday to re-assure me that she was having the house. I enjoyed the holiday even more after that welcome news.

We all found it so much more convenient once we had moved. I only had to cross the road and walk up Wharf Road to work. Our daughter had a much shorter distance to walk along to Alfgaer School, and our son attended Churchfields School not far away at all. All in all, we felt we had made the right decision in moving and were very happy. We all loved the house and the convenience of living just a five-minute walk into Rugeley.

The house was very roomy and we were able to spread ourselves around; we revelled in it. Now the children were growing up it was good for them to have their own space, plus as well as the upstairs toilet and bathroom, there was a shower and toilet downstairs, luxury indeed.

Christmas-time was always very busy at the bakery and I will always remember the girls saying in the run up to it that they never wanted to see another mince pie again as long as they lived. It was the same when Easter approached with the hot cross buns; even I was fed up with seeing and smelling them so I knew how the girls felt.

For a few years, things went well and life got even better if possible; the children were growing up fast, we began to have a few luxuries.

Next door to us lived a very nice couple named Charlie and Dorothy. They were much older than we were, but we struck up a good friendship. Dorothy was a wonderful cook and would invite us round for coffee, then she would put on an enormous spread of homemade bread, sausage rolls, cakes, and biscuits, so you didn't want anything else to eat for at least two days after. They were such a nice friendly couple that even when we moved, they kept in touch. Eventually they moved to Brereton, but our friendship continued. Poor Charlie died from leukaemia and Dorothy moved to a flat not too far from us, and we remained friends until she died in 2004.

When we lived next door to Charlie and Dorothy, we sent away for tickets to go and watch BBC's *Pebble Mill at One*, which was screened at the television studios in Edgbaston, just the other side of Birmingham City Centre. We enjoyed it so much that we then obtained free tickets to go and watch *The Basil Brush Show*, we all thoroughly enjoyed watching these shows and wished we had time to go and see more, but family and work commitments prevented it.

Our children enjoyed the show *Crossroads* and one day while we were in Birmingham, they persuaded me to take them to see the ATV studios. The door attendant was very nice and we all had a good old chat. The children were fascinated by all the information he gave them about the show. He was so friendly that he even rang Noele Gordon's secretary, Ellen Neil-Sturgess; she came down from her office, had a chat with us, and took us up to the canteen for coffee and cakes. She was a lovely lady. The youngsters were thrilled and afterwards as we were walking back into town, they told me where the next episode was being filmed so we then hiked over to Bradford Street and climbed a few flights of stairs to satisfy their curiosity. They were bowled over after peering through the glass window on the doors, seeing their favourite actors. Of course, they were quickly spotted and we were politely ejected. As we were walking down the stairs, Noele Gordon was in the lift going down so we missed seeing her, but we did meet the young man who played Sandy; he was a lovely person. We also met quite a few other well known characters that day, and on reaching home the children declared it was the best day out they had ever had. I didn't get the shopping I had originally gone for, but it didn't matter; just seeing their happy smiling faces was enough. To this day, my son still has the signed photographs.

This set them off on, 'Let's go and meet the Celebs if we can.' I hoped this phase wouldn't last long.

They did get to meet a few; Paul enjoyed meeting Bucks Fizz after one of their concerts. He had written and received a reply saying he could go backstage after the show. He has a nice signed photograph of that, taken backstage at The Odeon Cinema in Birmingham. It was below freezing outside waiting for him, and I desperately hoped he wouldn't be long.

He also went to meet Ruth Madoc when she was in pantomime. She is a lovely woman and told him how to get into show business if ever he decided to follow that road.

One of Paul's favourite television programs was *Take the High Road*. He wrote to Scottish TV and was delighted to be invited to the studios. One day we got on the train at Birmingham New Street, and travelled up to Scotland, and eventually found ourselves in the studios. We were treated like royalty and escorted round, treated to lunch, and even offered an overnight stay at a hotel so that we could be taken the next day to watch the show being filmed. Having gone ill equipped to say the least, with just our fare and snack money in hand, I had to decline. I was very disappointed for Paul, but at least we had been and visited the studios.

Around that time, we started to visit Butlin's Holiday Camp at Minehead for our summer holiday. We went in the August of the long hot summer of 1976, it was scorching hot for those two weeks and we thoroughly enjoyed ourselves and vowed to return. The day we left the weather broke on our homeward journey, and we had a cracker of a thunderstorm.

We visited Butlins many times after that holiday, but when it was sold on it quickly lost its appeal and we stopped going. At least we all have happy memories of those distant summers.

1980s

We got to know another family who lived further along the Brereton Road and it turned out that their parents owned a holiday cottage at a place called Meols, near Hoylake in the Wirral. They offered us the use of it for a small fee. We took them up on their kind offer and one weekend we packed up our belongings, and with Connie our black German Shepherd dog in the tail end of the car and children in the back, off we headed to what was to be the start of magical holidays and weekends for years to come.

The first time we went to Meols, it rained and rained and we came home early, as we didn't enjoy ourselves. Nevertheless, something tugged at us to return and I am so glad we did as the magic of the cottage and being a stone's throw from the seafront grabbed us all and we fell totally in love with the area.

One thing I loved to watch were the little boats bobbing up and down on the sea, exactly how the artist Lowry portrayed them in his paintings.

There were some wonderful walks and places to visit and as we returned home, we always planned our next visit.

On one of our visits, Paul and I went on the train to Liverpool. Alighting at the station, we couldn't see an exit, only a lift. Along with many thousands of other people I detest lifts, but somehow I found myself crammed into a huge lift with hundreds, at least it seemed like hundreds of other people. Well I bottled it and grabbed Paul, I screamed, 'Let us out, let us out.' I pushed my way through the crowd. After I had recovered, we found the staircase to the exit. It was steep to say the least, but I would rather climb the stairs of the Eiffel Tower than get in a lift.

We would take the train to Southport some days and have a wonderful day out looking round the shops and exploring the area. Birkenhead and West Kirby were also favourite haunts. The people were always so friendly and helpful, you only had to ask them for directions and all of a sudden, you had found a new best friend. They were great. Now with the passing of time, we wonder sometimes why we didn't sell up and move to Hoylake years ago. Still, we can always sit back, wonder what could have been, and rewrite our lives

We also enjoyed day trips to London and had many interesting walks around the city. The rail fares were surprisingly cheap, but the shop prices were really high. I remember buying a Coca Cola in one of the cafes in the 1970s and nearly fell off my stool when I had to pay 75 pence. I wonder what it is now.

I went with a young woman from the Imperial Garage one Saturday to watch the Trooping of the Colour. The crowds were huge and we would have seen more if we had stayed at home and watched it on the television. It was unbelievably hot that day and we were glad to catch the train home.

On another occasion, I took the children to London on a cheap day return and unfortunately, there was an IRA bomb scare so most of the city was cordoned off. We even stood watching the police activities from behind the barriers. It was only later that I realised how stupid I had been to stand watching. If there had been a bomb, we would have caught the full blast and been injured or killed. I berated myself for months afterwards at putting the children's lives in danger.

Remembering the bomb scare made me think of the bomb at the Tavern in the Town public house in Birmingham. Hearing it on the morning news, I thought, 'Thank goodness Mom and Dad are okay.' I was thinking of John's parents, never thinking that they would be in town that night, but Mom was. Mom later told me that she had gone with a friend to watch Swan Lake at the Theatre Royal. Thank goodness, they were safe; they heard the blast and were caught up in the confusion, of course. Awful, awful time for the victims, their families, Birmingham, and its citizens.

We lived in Brereton at that time, one of our friends was Irish, and he came and apologised for what had happened. Of course, it wasn't his fault, but we understood how he felt and it took him a good while to return to his usual self.

Now while writing this, London has been attacked, more memories that are so awful are made. Another shocking day imprinted on the nation's memory.

Deciding to stretch my wings, I took Helen on a trip to France via the hovercraft; it was one of the weekend trips were you travel in the early hours of a Saturday morning and return in the early hours of Sunday morning. The trip out wasn't bad at all; John dropped us at New Street station in Birmingham and we caught the train to Dover then the coach to the Hovercraft. It was a very short trip across to France and we both enjoyed it. A coach picked us up and ferried us to the hypermarket, the trip along the coast road was wonderful, seeing the white sands and blue, blue sea; we were surprised at the number of statues on the cliffs and would have liked the journey to have continued. After walking around the hypermarket, we travelled to Boulogne. Nobody thought to tell us that the shops close at midday on Saturdays and we found it quite boring, also tiring due to our early start.

On the overnight train back to New Street, we were packed like sardines in a can in the carriage. There was no way I could fall asleep as there were people's arms and legs stretched out everywhere, and it seemed as if everyone was snoring. Thank goodness, John was waiting to meet us and take us home. It took us a few days to recover, but it was well worth the experience.

Not long afterwards, having caught the travel bug, I took Paul to Guernsey to stay for a couple of days with my parents.

I was impressed with the friendliness of the people in St. Peter's Port, they spoke French, but as soon as they realised we were English they replied in our language and were polite. It was different from when I was in France; I was quite horrified at how rude the shopkeepers were and if we hadn't stood our ground, we would never have been served. I have been told that this is quite normal for the towns near the ports; inland it is a different story as the people are quite overwhelming in their friendliness.

Driving across the island of Guernsey, you could stop outside the farms and pick up a bag of tomatoes or whatever was on sale, pop the money in the box, and off you would drive; very trusting, and lovely to buy fruit and vegetables so fresh.

The holiday was soon over and sadly, we boarded the plane. I wasn't worried about the short flight back to Birmingham Airport; I had enjoyed the flight over to the island, as the views were superb. We seemed to skim across the water, which was glistening like jewels with the morning sun on it; we landed briefly at Jersey then skimmed across to Guernsey.

All went well on the return flight and coming into land, we flew across the motorway and I wondered if John was still driving along it as he was meeting us. It was then the trouble started, the pilot missed his landing and had to go round again, everything seemed to be going pear-shaped and people were being sick and some were even crying. I thought, 'My goodness, if we get out of this okay, I will never make this trip again.' The planes to the Channel Isles are quite small, I think then they called them the coach plane or something similar and seeing the motorway tipping beneath us did my nerves no good whatsoever; to this day I have never returned. On reflection, it is a little silly as I have never heard of an accident ever happening with the airline, but perhaps it's wise not to tempt fate.

1984

We were making plans for our first holiday abroad when disaster struck in the shape of the pit strike. Who would have thought the men would strike, not I.

To earn extra money, I had to leave Hindleys, and I tried my hand at running a small mobile snack bar. I did this for a few weeks with a girl I befriended at Hindleys. Her name was Pam and she drove one of the delivery vans. Pam and her husband, Dave, ran a laundrette that was next to the snack bar along the Horse Fair. Dave was a lorry driver and was away a lot so when I struck up a friendship with Pam, she would come and have a coffee and chat with me to help pass the time. When I mentioned the snack bar, she offered to come and help out; we had quite a few laughs cooking sausages and beef burgers by the roadside, but unfortunately, I couldn't get a trader's license so in the end I had to sell the van on; I was so disappointed as I could see how money could be made quite quickly once you were established.

Left with no work and no money coming in, things looked bleak. There were absolutely no jobs available due to the pit strike so I decided to set up a mobile cleaning business with just myself on the books. I quickly found work out of the area.

The first job I found was on the way to Stafford working for a doctor and his wife three mornings a week. I then answered an advert for a nanny-cum-helper for a consultant and his wife just five minutes away from my doctor's job. They were very flexible with their hours and things began to fall into place. I was fortunate enough to find work with a lady who lived at Milford, who allowed me to work in the afternoons. So my weekdays were full, but we still needed as much money as we could find due to the strike. I stayed with those three women for quite a few years; they were all lovely women and treated me with respect, not just as the hired help. I still exchange Christmas cards with one of them.

I then read an advertisement for a bank that needed a cleaner for a few hours through the week during the evenings. I was fortunate to land this job and although life was very busy, we were still short of money. John helped with the evening work, and I then found a job weekends and so it went on, working more and more just to survive the strike. Eventually, we had to admit defeat and rather than lose the house altogether, we reluctantly decided to move. My thoughts about Arthur Scargill are unprintable. I blamed him for our troubles.

We quickly sold the house and I found a semi-detached house in Leathermill Lane. It was in a state when we moved in and I felt very bitter for a long time, and found it as hard to settle as I had done when we had first moved to Brereton. We moved into the house on 23/4/82.

I carried on with my cleaning jobs, as work had become scarce plus even though I was working long hours, I was my own boss and if I thought I was being used by one of my employers, I quickly left and found another job.

I remember one woman who I started to work for expected me to sit on the upstairs window ledges and clean the outside windowpanes. No way was I doing that, so after a brief discussion I took my leave.

Another woman expected me to put the ladders up outside and clean the upstairs windows. I refused to do that. This particular woman had a huge round carpet in front of the fire in the lounge. I took it up to clean underneath it and found a two-pence piece placed strategically right in the centre under it. I knew she was checking up on me.

One day I took my break and decided to go round to the local Kwik Save to get something for my lunch; as I sat in my car I glanced up to see an elderly man waving his stick in the air and pointing to his watch. He had obviously been primed to keep his eye on me to make sure I worked my hours. I was furious, but determined to work my two weeks so I could pick up my pay. This woman left me lists and lists of jobs to do. I nicknamed her Mrs List. The day before my pay was due, I went to Kwik Save again and looking on the notice board, I wasn't surprised to see she had advertised for another cleaner. I pitied her next victim and was quite certain no one would last very long in the job.

Not long after moving into Leathermill Lane, we acquired a home-based CB Radio. At first, as with anything new it was great fun chatting away to people over the airwaves and at one time, it seemed everyone who was anyone had one.

Of course, this was before mobile phones and computers so having a CB radio in your car was a huge asset should you break down and if you were within range, you could contact home if you were going to be late. It certainly made me feel safer.

One morning on my way to work, I placed the CB into position in my car, realised I had forgotten my bag and popped back into the house for it. Driving along the Wolseley Road towards work, I reached down to turn the CB on and was shocked to realise it wasn't there. I pulled into the roadside and had a good look round the car – even under the seats – it was nowhere to be found. I realised slowly that in the couple of minutes when I had popped back into the house, someone had stolen it.

I was so angry at my stupidity, also with the thief; obviously, an opportunist theft, but how quickly they had acted, and it was unbelievable to me that in that short space of time it had gone for good.

Where I lived at that time was by no means a busy road, after all there were only five houses and a garage, plus it was quite early in the morning when the theft happened. I certainly hadn't seen anyone about but they had obviously been watching me.

It taught me a lesson and I never left the car unlocked again, it was a hard way to learn but nevertheless, I did.

I really missed the CB, but John soon set me up with another one and I quickly had 'my ears on' as they said in CB language.

The CB radio theft reminded me of another occasion; when we lived in the flat above the Co-op shop, a couple of 'friends' popped in to see me one evening. They were in no way related, more like friends of friends and it was quite by accident that they visited me at the same time that particular evening.

When they arrived, I had been sorting my handbag out and had left my wage packet (wages weren't paid into the bank in those days) and purse on the arm of a chair. We sat talking when the doorbell went again; I popped out to answer it and it was Pauline, my sister. The other two visitors didn't stay long and after they had gone, I checked my wages and to my horror, there was a chunk of money missing from the wage packet and my purse. I was embarrassed by my stupidity and realised there was no way I could accuse either one of my 'acquaintances', strangely enough they never visited me again.

On my afternoons off, I would catch the bus into Birmingham at least once a week. I enjoyed my shopping trips and liked to visit the Museum, Art Gallery and any psychic fairs that might be on. My interest had certainly continued over the years, and one day I hoped to investigate it further. I would never have guessed how I would be given the opportunity to do this.

Through CB Radio, I met a group of people, known as breakers, who ran a club and they invited us along. One of the men, Jim, worked in Birmingham and John asked him if he would give me a lift occasionally into the city. He agreed so whenever I wanted a lift home if he thought he was going to finish on time, he agreed to pick me up. On full days off, Jim would pick me up and drop me at my mother-in-laws in Kings Heath. As John's Granddad lived next door, I would pop in and visit him as well.

John's granddad was very creative; to help fill his days after he had retired and Granny Palmer had died; Pop made himself a large frame, stretched a piece of canvas over it, and then proceeded to make wool rugs. He even made an appliance just the right length to cut the wool to the correct size. he created many different designs as he went along. I never saw him work from a chart and I found it intriguing to watch him work.

If I could, I would buy him some wool if I thought it was suitable; he was always grateful for my offerings so the wool must have been okay.

Pop was always doing wiring jobs around his rooms and there were wires running here there and everywhere; I often thought he would blow himself up one day, but he must have known what he was doing because everything kept on working.

One Friday I popped in to see him and was surprised to find him chatting away to a man who was a complete stranger to me. The man was talking away to Pop and I had difficulty in understanding him, as he had a very strong Irish accent. Pop intimated this man was his friend, so reluctantly after about half an hour, I left them to their chat. I felt very uneasy about this, but there was nothing I could do.

A few days later, I learnt to my horror that Pop had been robbed by this man, and really I wasn't too surprised, as I had felt distrustful of him. From what I recall, the man had started to talk to Pop in the village and Pop invited him along to his house for a cup of tea. I often wished I had stayed with him that day, but then it was there it was going to happen and you can't alter fate.

Then later on in the day, I would go back into town shopping and meet Jim near Marks and Spencer's and have a lift home.

So the years passed and the house began to take shape; we extended the kitchen and added a conservatory, generally making the house our own. I came to love living there.

We had lovely neighbours. One of them, Herbert Beresford, lived next door. He was a bachelor and spent a lot of his time in Wales helping at a friend's caravan site.

In between his trips to Wales, Herbert would tidy his garden and grow vegetables; he would phone me quite often to say he had placed some beans over the fence for me, or some other vegetable. He was a good friend.

I really admired Herbert he was a lot older than us, but age was no barrier as he had a young attitude to life and lots of energy.

He supported a number of charities; giving of his time freely. Nothing seemed too much trouble for him. He was also a very intelligent man and was blessed with a photographic memory. He only had to read something once and it was there for all time in his memory. I was very upset when I heard he had died suddenly on one of his trips to Wales in the late 1990s.

My daughter married a man from Uttoxeter and lived with her mother-in-law for a short while in Rocester. They came to see me one day to say they were expecting their first child. I was delighted and then realised we would be elevated to grandparents. I thought, like millions of others, we weren't old enough, but we were.

One day I was working at the consultant's house when my daughter came to the door. She was quite heartbroken; the child, a boy, had Spina Bifida. They had told her that the child wouldn't live and she was advised to have a termination. A terrible decision had to be taken; I immediately left work, and she travelled home with me in my car, and her husband behind in his mother's car. A great sadness descended on the house for the next few weeks and we all prayed for a miracle, but of course, miracles rarely happen except in fairy tales. We kissed little Stewart farewell and the only comfort we derived was that he had been spared further pain and suffering.

Our son had been working on the Isle of Man and he came home to lend what support he could. Together as a family, we got through that bad time.

A couple of months afterwards, Helen came across for the day. She had booked an appointment with a clairvoyant who worked from an empty shop not far from where I lived. I went along with her and purely out of interest, decided to have a reading myself.

They say certain events can change your life and that reading changed mine. I found it fascinating and a few days later, something the lady reader told me came true. I immediately booked another appointment and watched her as she read the Tarot Cards. I was intrigued as to how she could derive so much information from a set of picture cards.

Helen had not been impressed with her reading, as she had expected to derive some comfort from it. However, she was expecting another baby by then so she wasn't over bothered.

We went into Birmingham and I popped into a bookshop and quickly found the department where they sold tarot cards. I knew enough by then to know that it was advisable to buy the cards you were most drawn to. After a time I made my choice and bought two packs. On arriving home, I began to teach myself the basics. On another foray into Birmingham, I bought a book about Tarot. I still have it to this day. Every reader should have one. Over the following months, I taught myself all I could and practiced readings on my family and friends, with pleasing results.

My mother was so against it, but after giving her a reading, she quickly became a big fan.

Eventually, I placed a small advertisement in our local paper and was shocked at the reaction. I had dozens of calls, but I made it a rule that I would only see three or four people a week.

I realised I had a gift and was determined to use it to help others. I started getting regular clients, and gradually gave up my cleaning jobs, and did a couple more readings a week to make my wages up.

Sometimes when I was giving a reading, a client would tell me a ghost story and rather than forget it, I began to jot them down, with the client's permission of course. Somewhere at the back of my mind, the idea for a book was beginning to form. I was asked to give talks, but turned the offers down. I was far to shy to do that.

My daughter and I had also started a small ironing company. She had moved to Rugeley not far from where we lived, and having young children, it was difficult for her to obtain work outside the home. I began to think everything was going right for us, as the ironing business was a success.

I had grown to love where we lived; to my surprise, I preferred it to our house along the Brereton Road.

The few afternoons I had to myself, I would take my dog walking on Cannock Chase. I loved the peace and quiet to be found once away from the main tourist areas. Watching the deer roaming free never ceased to delight me. There weren't many times that I didn't see them when I was on one of my hikes. Once the recession hit the country, the Chase became more popular as people having more time on their hands discovered this beautiful area right on their doorsteps.

I remember in the very hot summer of 1976, the Forestry was asking for firewatchers. Due to the risk of forest fires, the whole of Cannock Chase was closed. We applied and were accepted. That was truly a memorable experience walking across Cannock Chase with our dog, not seeing a single soul; it was a bit like having your own country estate I should think. I was quite sad when it re-opened and as far as I can recollect, it has only ever been closed to the public once since, this was when the foot and mouth epidemic swept the country a few years ago. The Chase is a fascinating place and I am always impressed by the ever-changing seasons.

I still went into Birmingham when I could, and had lifts now and then from Jim. When John's parents went to stay at their cottage in Wales, I would visit Pop Pops, John's granddad, next door and have a chat and make sure he was okay.

Some afternoons I would go to the theatre to see a ballet, as I was the only one in the family who enjoyed it, or I would visit the cinema to watch a film.

One time I even went to the Motor Show at the NEC. I remember feeling a little tired and sat down on a chair to have a rest, and promptly fell asleep. I don't know what people made of me, but I felt very embarrassed on waking up and realising what had happened.

A strange thing started occurring when I was shopping and out and about in Birmingham; I began to long to be on one of my walks with the dogs across the Chase. Something I never thought would happen. I loved Birmingham with every bone in my body; how strange it was for me to miss the Chase, me, a townie. I realised I didn't want to move back to Birmingham. I had fallen in love with the peace and quiet of the countryside.

As the years passed, John and I would go and open up the cottage (Bryntegan) after the winter for his parents. I fell in love with it all over again. We would mow the lawns and tidy the inside, but there was so much land we only had time to do the one side, as by that time of year, (May) the grass was very long indeed.

We were always fortunate with the weather in that it never rained on the day we went. At the top of the steps leading down into the garden were two stone lions, the top step became known as Carol's step, as it was where I would sit and have my morning coffee and take in the wonderful scenery. The lions now stand in my garden.

The first time I really felt the magic of Bryntegan was one May morning just as the sun stole across the sky and lit everything up; it was truly a wonderful experience. It felt as if every age met in that one brief moment of time. Since then I have felt it many more times in that garden. One day while working in the garden, I sensed that there was someone behind me, instinctively I knew it wasn't John and glanced behind me. I saw an elderly man dressed in soldier's uniform hurrying down the garden steps. I blinked and the man disappeared. How strange, I thought, my heart skipping a beat realising I had seen a ghost.

The cottage has a mention in Kilvert's Diary, referred to as the 'dear little shed on the hill'. Of course, it has been extended over the years by John's parents, who bought it around forty years ago, sadly no longer owned by them, as it had to be sold when John's dad became ill. I am so glad that I felt the magic of Bryntegan, and miss the days we spent there.

Late 1980s-1990s

Time marched on and one day I had to go into Birmingham to collect a book that I had ordered. I had a lift into the city from our friend Jim, and he said he would pick me up as he had to leave Birmingham around two o'clock to go to a job on the Staffordshire moorlands so he could drop me in Rugeley. I told him not to bother as I could easily catch the bus home. He argued that it was no trouble to him to give me a lift. Despite my protests and better judgement, I gave in and agreed, thanking him. 'I will meet you at about two o'clock in the usual place.' I really didn't want a lift as that day for some reason or other I wanted to go home on the bus.

He picked me up and we were just leaving a council depot, I think it was on or near the Smallbrook Ringway, and we were going round a roundabout on the way out of Birmingham when he suddenly shouted that there was a car leaving the car park on the left and he couldn't stop. I was looking down at the time at something in my bag so didn't see it happening, but I felt and heard the metal crashing against metal; The accident is obviously a memory that I will live with forever.

Of course, I was badly shaken up and taken to hospital in Birmingham against my will, as I just wanted to go home. I had severe whiplash and I still suffer the after-effects to this day. Fortunately, the driver of the other vehicle and Jim weren't hurt. The cars were very badly damaged.

The injury led me to losing my ironing business; I had started this a few months previously with my daughter and it was becoming highly successful. I found movement extremely painful and I had weekly physiotherapy for a number of years.

As mentioned earlier I also lost many of my memories and to this day suffer the after effects physically of the accident.

I consider myself lucky though as things could have turned out a lot worse.

Not to be beaten though, I decided to devote more time to writing my first book of ghost stories, I had been jotting down the stories people had told me over the years so I thought perhaps the accident had been a sign in some way that this was what I was meant to do. I was concerned as to whether I could really pass muster as a writer, and I approached an Irish Magazine asking if they would be interested in an article on ghostly happenings. They replied saying they would and I was truly happy when the article was accepted. That increased my confidence and I wrote quite a few more articles about various matters, and also items on crafts and these were accepted in many magazines. It was all very cheering after what had happened, and I pressed ahead with my first book: *Mystical Staffordshire.*

It was after I had published my first book that I became even more interested in the supernatural and I began reading books on the subject and also going to see clairvoyants, mediums, and visiting psychic events. One of the ladies I visited recorded her reading for me and on listening to it back home, I must admit I was sceptical saying, 'None of this will happen.' Well I certainly had to eat my words, as over the years, much of what she predicted has happened. Even when she predicted that I would use equipment to do with radio; I did go on local radio a few times and afterwards, I remembered the predictions.

My main reason for visiting the mediums was to see if I could receive a message from the world of 'Spirit'. I never did despite many visits. When the mediums I visited didn't get in touch with anyone, I was told that I was blocking the way. I couldn't accept that as I was desperately trying to receive a genuine sign that there was life after death, albeit completely different from the here and now. I somehow imagined that maybe a parallel existence ran alongside us, and that with just a little help, we could step over into that world. That is if someone could give us the key; it was one of my many imaginings that has come to nothing, of course.

One gentleman medium who I visited in Birmingham for a reading one morning told me he had my mother trying to talk to me. I nearly fell off my chair with shock, as I had been chatting to my mom a couple of hours ago on the telephone. She lived in Guernsey and I was astonished to say the least when he said that he had her in the world of spirit. When I pointed this out, he quickly changed Mom into Grandma. I lost interest then and gave up my search for a while.

There are a couple of readings amongst the many I had that I will never forget.

Whilst in Birmingham, I went to visit a 'medium'; he had a small rented room in an old building in Digbeth. I went to see him, but really didn't learn a lot from the reading. This was one of the times that I wasn't meeting Jim for a lift home so rushing for the bus through the Pallasades, I thought I had better pay a visit to the toilet. I put my bag on the floor, hearing someone running into the toilet, I thought, 'She's desperate.' But then I saw my bag disappearing under the door; I screamed, but too late it had gone, and by the time I had made myself respectable, she or he had gone, of course. The people in the arcade were kind to me, rang the police, and I was taken to Digbeth Road Police Station. They took my details and rang John, who hurried over to collect me; it wasn't our day as a stone hit the windscreen and smashed the screen!

What shocked me was how much of my personal stuff I carried around with me; new reading glasses, over a hundred pounds in cash, credit cards, etc. The most valuable thing had no monetary value whatsoever, it was a brooch Mom had given to me that had belonged to my Grandma Davies, it was always in my purse. We never recovered anything and no doubt, once they had taken the valuables, the bag would have been thrown into a canal somewhere.

After I had settled down, I thought back to my reading from the medium and realised that he hadn't mentioned my being robbed at all. Thinking back to that summer, I recalled going to see a gypsy reader in Wales, she read the playing cards. I recalled her telling me to look after my money; in fact, she mentioned it twice. Then I have always believed we can't stop the bad things happening, but we can make good happen.

I went to Lichfield Spiritualist Church for a few years, and made some good friends there. When they began to move away, I lost touch and concentrated on collecting my ghost stories and writing my books.

I also gave a few readings from time to time to 'old customers' who kept in touch.

What amazed me about giving card readings was some people's attitude to paying. I never charged a lot for my readings, but enough to give me a sense of self-worth and also to cover the cost of replacing my cards, tea, coffee, and time. I well remember a hairdresser asking me in Birmingham what I did for a living. When I told her, she was very interested and asked me questions. When I mentioned I made a small charge, she was shocked. I asked her, 'Do you get paid for going to work?' Of course she did, so why should I not be paid for my work? Unlike most professions, clairvoyants cannot work to a schedule, as they have to fit in with their clients. Perhaps you may only have one booking on any particular day. It may be booked for the afternoon to fit in with the client. If the client doesn't show, then you have lost a whole day when you could have been gainfully employed doing other things. I well understand now why some readers charge a deposit before accepting a booking. No one minds if the appointment is cancelled, but to just not turn up is extremely rude.

A charge is not wrong when you consider you have to work some evenings or weekends. You don't receive sickness benefit, holiday payments, or overtime, and you are giving someone the most precious gift you can: your time. It is not all about just giving a reading; it is about listening and being sympathetic to someone who undoubtedly needs someone to talk to. I think you can safely say that 95% of people who visit clairvoyants are in some kind of trouble, have no one who will listen to them, and need to know when things are going to turn around for them. The majority of clairvoyants will give up whole afternoons for someone who is unhappy. Where else can these people go in today's busy society? Doctors definitely don't have the time, neither do Social Services. Families and friends are too close to hear their private thoughts. By visiting a clairvoyant, they know they will be heard in a non-judgemental way, and be given a good idea as to when their circumstances are going to improve.

I did visit many mediums in my quest, and places where mediums work from the stage. I had no messages.

I asked one lady medium if she could sense anyone from the spirit world with me, but she replied, 'No, but do go and see someone else, they might be able to help you.' I was impressed to say the least by her honesty and have carried on having readings from her for a number of years. She gives me readings for the future and is quite helpful with past lives.

Eventually though, I was honest with myself that I was never going to receive a message from anyone.

Instinct tells me that my sister Pauline is often with me, never anyone else.

I feel as if Pauline has been by me more in these last few months urging me on to finish this book, saying, 'Come on get on with it.' Of course it could be my imagination that she is with me. I would like to think she is and always will be.

During the years when I read the cards for the public, I was asked to go to a public house across the Chase; they were putting on a show. The public house had a large room with a stage, and they asked if I would be interested in doing some clairvoyance. To this day, I don't know where I got the courage from, but I agreed.

Of course, I was very nervous and told the man who was presenting the show that I would tell him what I 'saw' and he could relay it to the persons concerned. I gave a percentage of the fee to charity and knew it would work for me, and thank goodness it did. I was overwhelmed all night with offers of work, and that night was the start and finish of my stage career. I know it wouldn't go my way if I took on regular work and was quite happy with that one appearance.

I have done other charity work using my 'gift' and have been pleased to do so.

So for all my delving, pondering, and discussions, do I believe in life after death? I don't know; I would like to think that we meet up with our loved ones again, awful to think this is it and we never get a chance to ever give them a hug and say, 'I love you.' Best to say it now and have no regrets, as we never know, do we?

Writing about the stage reminded me of when my son was very young, he became really star-struck and decided he was going to be a singer when he grew up. We were at

123

what was once the British Legion along the main A51 road, not far from Lodge Road, Brereton, though it's now a housing estate. The organisers were asking for people in the audience to get up on stage and do a 'turn'. Without a second's hesitation, Paul jumped up, ran on stage, and sang a song. He got a good round of applause and like me, has never volunteered since. He was very young at the time and nerves didn't come into it.

Around this time, Paul developed a phobia about going to the barbers; I tried every which way I could to persuade him to go; in the end I said I would cut it for him. I did and he went willingly to the barbers every time I mentioned he needed to go after that.

A little about my sister Pauline

Pauline eventually re-married when she moved back to Birmingham and in time, she moved to Cornwall. Unfortunately, she hated living there, saying it was like being on a permanent holiday and she couldn't settle. The next thing I knew she was moving to Scotland. At this time, she was eight months pregnant with twins and she had to do all the work of packing on her own as her husband, was working abroad.

Soon after the move to Ayrshire, she had twin girls. For a while, she seemed more settled and occasionally travelled down to stay with us at the various houses we lived in. I loved having her and the girls to visit. When she lived in Kilwinning, she ran a hairdressing business, then they moved to a larger house in Largs and she owned two shoe shops. In time, she gave these up, and her marriage failed. They divorced and she opened a boarding house with her new partner, Vernon, who was a chef. She was with him for quite a few years and they decided to get engaged. They bought the ring ready for the big party they had planned for the following day. Tragedy struck that same night; Pauline woke up to find Vernon dead in bed beside her. He had suffered a fatal stroke. This hit her even harder than her second divorce and I was concerned for her health, as she seemed to be on the edge of a nervous breakdown.

At one time when we lived in Brereton, she had seriously thought about buying a house nearby. I always regret her not doing this because after Vernon died, she really went to pieces and started drinking heavily. There was nothing anyone could do. She wasn't a happy drunk. The more she had the more bitter she became. This period lasted a long time and I worried about her. She had suffered from stomach ulcers and had lost part of her stomach in major surgery some years previously. Pauline also had to attend hospital regularly as she had kidney trouble. I worried that drinking as she was, would only make her worse.

Then a few years down the line, she said she had given up the drink. I was more than happy to have the old Pauline back and prayed she would not start drinking again. A few months later, in December 1996, I was shocked when she was rushed into hospital. Despite many tests, the doctors couldn't find what was wrong with her. She came home and I phoned her the next day, as it was also her birthday on the 17th. She said she was okay, but was having trouble eating. Obviously, this worried me a great deal and I said I would call her at Christmas. I never spoke to my sister again. She was rushed into hospital Christmas Eve. I kept ringing her new partner, who repeatedly assured me that she was fine. I knew she couldn't be, as I know they don't keep you in hospital over Christmas unless you are extremely ill. Nevertheless, he said she was doing fine. That was on the Sunday. Monday, New Year's Eve in the early hours Pauline died. What a tragedy, to die so young.

She was one of the people who encouraged me in my writing and particularly this book; she felt that the story should be written down and was always asking how it was coming along. In turn, I would ask her to write her memories down as she had a far better memory than I have. She never did and I really thought I would never achieve my aim of getting as much down on paper as I have. Unfortunately, the car accident caused me to lose many of my memories, but I am thankful I have noted down as much as I can remember.

Despite everything, she had so much pride and even slept in her car when she lost her home; she never told me until she had got back on her feet. If only I had known, I would have helped her.

After she died, there were quite a few times when I sensed she was near.

For a long, long time afterwards, I thought I saw her driving her car around Rugeley; every woman driver looked like Pauline to me. I have since discovered this happens to many people when they lose a loved one.

Now I have no need to visit mediums to try to get in 'touch' with the other side, I just accept that she is with me and it's enough.

It was strange how Pauline came to meet Maureen Carroll who is a second cousin to us.

Maureen had lived with her husband, Ron, in Greenland Road, Selly Park, Birmingham for some time, when Pauline and Peter became their third set of neighbours. The lady that owned the house was a friend of Maureen's grandmother's friends.

The following is what Maureen wrote to me.

'I cannot remember how we found out we were related, but we seemed to hit if off right away and we went out and about together. Then Ron and I moved to Tamworth, and Pauline and Peter followed not long after. We went on holiday together and enjoyed it, but Pauline's relationship was already beginning to show the cracks.

After a while, we began to drift apart and led our separate lives as by now, I had had my first child, Paul. Pauline and Peter became godparents, but we only occasionally had nights out.

After Pauline and Peter split up, we lost touch.

Peter Flynn re-married, but after a few meetings between him and his new wife, we lost touch.'

A few years ago, I was listening to Carl Chinn's radio show on BBC West Midlands and I heard a lady called Maureen speaking about the Giblen family; the names she was mentioning clicked as they were exactly the same names as some of our ancestors. I wrote to Carl Chinn and asked him if he could put me in touch with her.

After contact was made, Maureen and I exchanged quite a few letters and were getting on famously; one night our telephone rang and it was Maureen. She went on to say that she had been thinking about me the previous evening and had suddenly realised who I was. I had mentioned in one of my letters that my sister Pauline had died suddenly, and Maureen said she had suddenly tied our two names together and then everything had fallen into place. She had even met me many years before, what a small world it is! Maureen was shocked that Pauline had died, and we went on to discuss how strange it was that somehow despite everything, we were now in touch.

A little about Joy Arnall

Joy went to Colmore Road School then Kings Norton Grammar School in the 1950s; she would have been in a lower form than Pauline was. She eventually went to Birmingham College of Art and then Swansea University. Joy went on to teach art for a short while at Hereford College and she taught at Lady Hawkins School, Kingston, and Herefordshire.

She married Trevor in 1965 and they moved into a house called Rosedale that I remember had the most beautiful back garden stocked with flowers of every description. They didn't live at Rosedale for long as it was situated on a busy main road.

Trevor's father shared his money out amongst his family, saying he wanted them to have their inheritance whilst he was alive rather than dead!

Trevor and Joy then bought the farm Ffynnon Wen meaning, I am led to believe, 'running water'.

They lived there for many years, I did visit a time or two, but never felt comfortable in the farmhouse; to me the atmosphere was never right. It was many years later when I was chatting to John's mom that she remarked she'd also always felt uncomfortable in Ffynnon Wen, as had Dad. I was quite pleased to hear this as it confirmed my thoughts.

After John's uncle died - he owned, a cottage with a small amount of land in Wales - Joy and Trevor decided to move lock, stock, and barrel to the cottage. John's mom had moved to live with Joy and Trevor, as unfortunately, Father-in-law had sadly died.

As the big move was being planned, Joy discovered she had cancer of the kidney; apparently, there are two types of kidney cancer, one you recover from but the other is terminal; poor Joy discovered hers was the latter.

What a hectic time this was for them; Joy went into hospital to have her kidney removed more or less as the move was progressing, so overall it was a very stressful time.

Once they were all settled, Joy recovered from the operation really well and twelve months down the line, she rang full of excitement at the news she was clear of the cancer, wonderful!

It didn't seem like five minutes that I received an email from her saying that she was driving home from a day out when her head had seemed to explode in pain and flashing bright lights exploded at the back of her eyes. I wondered if she had a migraine.

Her doctor sent her back to the hospital where tests confirmed secondary cancer and a brain tumour.

Joy died within twelve months; the dream of living at the cottage in shreds. Another sister cruelly lost.

Rugeley – The changing scene

When we first came to live in Staffordshire, there was no regular bus service into Rugeley from Brereton; you either walked or you had to fork out for a taxi if you didn't own a car. We normally walked; it was a lovely little town when we came in the late 1960s. Traffic ran through the town centre, Woolworths had separate counters with women serving you whatever you wanted. There were ladies' clothes shops, wallpaper and paint shops, and a thriving market three times a week.

The wonderful corner shops have all but disappeared. There was a superb after-hours shop down Arch Street where you could pop in at any time in the evening, and Sunday afternoons they always seemed to have what you were looking for. The supermarkets have, of course, put paid to them, and I mourn their passing as they were such social places where you could have a nice friendly chat with the shopkeeper or meet a neighbour and while away a pleasant fifteen minutes. Now, it's all rush, rush, rush, and I never cease to be amazed at the amount of food people have in their shopping trolleys when they reach the checkout.

I remember the first supermarket to arrive in Rugeley. I had been in hospital and John told me that a large grocery store had opened whilst I was away; the following day after I had arrived home, he took me to 'Paddy's' in Brewery Street. It was the biggest grocery shop I had been in since living in Rugeley. All the goods were in huge cardboard boxes, and you had a trolley to wheel round to place your goods in. It was all very new to me and I wondered if it would catch on. Of course, it did and now the supermarkets reign supreme and are all-powerful.

Like many small towns, Rugeley has changed. With the pit closure, the town slowly died, now we have a plethora of charity shops, the markets are dying; all in all, the entire town is a sorry sight.

New estates are springing up all over the place and any green space is soon destroyed by another housing estate or block of flats.

My favourite walk across the Hagley Fields to the Chase has now all but disappeared; the farmer's fields that were there are now new housing estates. No doubt in the next ten years or so, all the fields will disappear to be replaced by houses; only memories and photographs of this once beautiful area will remain; and they call this progress.

I never thought I would settle down away from the city lights but I can honestly say if I had the choice I would not live in Birmingham now. It's changed beyond recognition and it would not feel like home.

Of course I'm still a Brummie, I always will be. I'm immensely proud of my Brummie roots they are forever embedded in the city streets of long ago.

Final Note

*Mom died June 18th, 2010. I was sent a copy of her will.

She wrote in 1976 that everything she owned, (should she survive my stepfather) should be shared between her children. She went on to name my three stepbrothers and one stepsister.

I'm so glad that my sister Pauline never saw the will. It would have destroyed her. It nearly did me.

I never wanted anything material from my Mother only her love, and she denied me that at the end.

132

Before our Wedding

Wedding day 21ˢᵗ March 1964

St. Kenelm's Church, Romsley

Trafalgar Square, London 1970s

Bryntegan, Colva 1950s

Me on Cannock Chase 1970s

Note my Dr Who scarf!

My son with Connie at Meols 1980s

John & Joy 1950s - Wales

Paul on Cobweb 1970s

Cannon Hill Park, Tulip Festival, 1960s

A very young John!

Muriel Arnall with Enid Blackwell
on the moors near Nevyn Wales

John's parent's wedding-September 1939

The view from Bryntegan cottage in the 1960s

Note the cars!

John & his father in the lane at Bryntegan 1950s

On the following page is a hand written account that my mother in law wrote in May 2011.

I have not altered it in anyway

Muriel Arnall wrote this on the 3rd November 2005

I was born on the 3rd July 1929, at Loveday Street Hospital, Birmingham. My first memory (I was 2 years of age), is of sitting on my father's lap wrapped in a twel having been bathed in the cooper, which was in a corner of the kitchen, its use was for boiling washing. This was at 24, Reservoir Road, Selly Oak, Birmingham. At the top of the garden there was a canal. My mother used to take me in my pushchair along the tow path to do her shopping, often passing horses pulling barges loaded with coal going into the canal basin in Birmingham.

Round about 3 years old, I went with my parent, Ellen and George Palmer to live at Ivy Cottage, Grovely Lane, Rednal, my father worked as a labourer on his parents, Alice and William Palmer's farm, Rose Cottage, just down the lane, I believe the farm belonged to John Palmer, Grandad's eldest brother who also lived there.

I had a brother Jack, younger than I, who lived with my grandparents on the farm. I have never been able to ascertain why this was. We used to play together as children, and were happy.

Oil Lamps, privy down the garden, water carried in buckets from a spring in the lane. Every Friday the oil cart came, also Faulks the grocer from Cotteridge. Grandma used to exchange eggs, chickens and home made butter, for other goods. I remember my brother and I turning the handle on the butter churn. It took ages for the butter to make.

I cannot remember my grandparents ever leaving the farm, not for a day. The kitchen quarry tiles were scrubbed on hand and knees every day, all coking was done on an open fire, the oven was on the side, all hot water boiled on a kettle hanging from a hook over the fire, but the most delicious cakes and puddings came from that over. There

148

was a deep well at the farm, and in the summer Grandma used to put meat in the bucked and lower it halfway down to keep cool. One day my brother and I took the hook off the handle, and the bucket hurtled to the bottom and splashed into the water. Were we in trouble, his punishment was the cane, which stood in a corner. Mine was to sit on a chair facing the clock.

I walked 2 miles to school, a church school at Cofton Hackett, where lots of the Palmers are buried. My first day at school, I remember very well. I wet my knickers, but my kind teacher, Miss Cope, soon put me to rights. In the middle of the classroom was a tortoise stove, coke fired for heating the room, she, Miss Cope used to make us mugs of cocoa in the winter, summer time, we'd get an apple, most the time, we had eaten our sandwiches on the way to school, so we had nothing until we got home again. Running up the lane , mom was always home to greet me, my first words were, 'mom, can I have a piece, this consisted of home made bread and jam, or dripping, sometimes lard. It certainly was organic from our own home fed pigs. I used to take my mug down to the cow shed, it was filled with milk, straight from the cow's udder, warm; today this would be called a deprived childhood, it was the best.

I learnt my nature, walking to school, seeing weasels, stoats, foxes, rabbits, learning the names of wild flowers, trees, birds, my greatest pleasure was a swing tied up in an apple tree. I still enjoy a swing and I'm 85 years old. I used to make believe, go off to far away places, no wireless, or television for me. There was great excitement one Christmas, dad bought a gramophone with 8 records, I think I was about 10 years old then. I have thought that today's children will never see Jack Frost on their bedroom window panes, beautiful lace pictures, no central heating in those days, either a brick warmed in the oven, or the oven shelf wrapped in an old blanket in my bed, which was a feather bed when Grandma plucked chickens, feathers were saved for beds and pillows. Along came the cat's whisker, first wireless, it had ear phones and only one person could hear, I had to keep quiet. I remember King George 5th dying, dad listening, an hourly bulletin of the King is gently passing away. It seemed a very long time for me to keep still.

I could read at the age of 4 years thanks to my mother. I still get great pleasure from reading even now.

Peg rugs were made during the winter, old coats, skirts and trousers, were cut into strips then pushed with the aid of a peg through a hole made into a hessian sack, which had probably contained cow nuts or grain. Hay making was a wonderful time for us children, I don't know about the adults, but bottles of cold tea, lemonade, home made bread and cheese, eaten out in the filed being allowed to ride on the cart horse bringing in the hay, they were such happy days. The one thing I couldn't bear was when the pig was killed. I wasn't allowed to witness this even, but I can still hear the squeals, I also helped after, by cleaning the chittlings, they were attached to a cold tap in the brew house, and you had to help squeeze the cold water through, but they were lovely to eat after, and also the pork scratching. I couldn't eat them now. I must mention the Lilac tree in the hedge, purple, still my favourite flower. Happy, happy childhood, as I'm writing this part on Nov 11th 2005 I can recall seeing a train stop on Nov 11th at 11.00 am 1927, it was a regular occurrence for everything to stop in those days. I must put on record the Lickey Hills, Rednal, so many happy hours, spent in the woods, along

150

Cofton Road. In the spring beech trees, bursting into bud, bluebell woods, anemones, birdsong, lazy days of summer. Autumn eating beech nuts, scuffing falling leaves as we wandered through woods on our way home from school. Life was hard for some, not for me, but I had darned socks, my brother patches on his trousers, but there were children without shoes in my class at school. I had good plain food, and was well cared for. It was a safe world. I could walk the lanes alone, without fear. There were about four murders a year and a special newspaper would be brought out. Those Halcyon days in the country came to an end when I was 12 years old. My mother had never settled, so we moved to a council house on an estate at Northfield, my only pleasure was a flush toilet.

Dad, had a job on the railway, he did enjoy his work. I've suddenly remembered fog; sometimes it was so thick you couldn't see where you were going.

Dad used to put detonators on the railway line to warn the train it was approaching a tunnel, they made a booming sound. One particular night mom and I went to take him a billy can of soup, but we never found him. We got ourselves lost in the thick fog, when we finally got back home, I was minus a shoe I had lost in the mud.

I've now got to fourteen, when I started work in a factory in Selly Oak. I enjoyed the company, and there I met my best friend Edna Sankey. I went through a very unhappy time, my father left home, and went to live with a woman called Louie. I was left to look after my mother, and my wages of four and sixpence a week had to feed us. After a year he came back home, but life was never the same. Lots of arguments between my parents, at the age of sixteen I met a boy with lovely auburn hair, name of Barrie,

151

we were married in 1939 Sep 30th, I was nineteen he was twenty. War had been declared with Germany so we got married by special license, nine weeks after his father died, we were left to care for his mother, no widow's pension then. Four weeks after the death of his father, Barrie was called up for the army, he joined the Royal Artillery regiment and I was left to look after his mother and sister, and also had to go to work. I was a conductress on the trams, (a clippie). Barrie came home on leave, but life was so full I can't remember, I can only remember air raids and bombs dropping night after night, his mother and I slept? In an air raid shelter in the garden until it got flooded, then we slept under the table in the kitchen with one dog, a cat and a canary, His sister had got married and gone to live at Kings Heath. Strange but there was such a feeling of comradeship amongst people, you shared thing, food, with complete strangers. In 1942, I had a baby boy, he was born in Selly Oak Hospital, and his father was allowed compassionate leave to see him.

Barrie was discharged from the army due to injury and we moved to Wales. Where he found work in Coway, these were happy days. We lived at Llamfairfechan overlooking the sea, for some reason we returned to Birmingam. And then went back to Wales to live at Nevin, Nefyn. We weren't made very welcome, The Welsh people were hostile towards us, except two who were very kind to me. I was living there alone with the children. Barrie had returned to Birmingham to find work., I can't think what at.

Eventually we moved back to the Midlands, partly because John was five and only Welsh was taught in the schools / We ended up in a lovely cottage at Catshill near Bromsgrove, where Barrie found work in Bromgrove, money was very short but the countryside was lovely. We had kind neighbours. Once again no work so back to Birmingham, where we lived at 39, Vicarage Road, Kings Heath. I'm proud of the fact that we eventually bought 39 and the adjoining 41, where my parents came to live.

My husband was a very kind person, allowing my parent to live at 41, paying rates for them, and not asking for rent, all repairs were cared for by him/ They lived a peaceful old age there, with us caring for them.

I found it very demeaning doing housework for them, and looking after Barrie's mother, and bringing up my own children, they weren't the hard work children seem to be today, but mine were taught discipline and respect. It's difficult to write it all down, lots have to stay in my memory.

Joy did well at school, she passed for Kings Norton Grammar school, and ended up at 18 going to Swansea University, trained to be an Art teacher, she finished training and got married.

John was mechanically minded he left Wheelers Lane School at 16, and went to work at the Coop garage a very quiet reserved boy. I've forgot to put in.

In 1959 we put all our saving £350.00 into buying a cottage, 'Bryntegan', we couldn't afford holiday, but had working ones, doing up our lovely country home, 75 miles from Kings Heath, we moved in complete with three orange boxes, 4 mugs, 4 plates, and lots of giggling. We dragged in an old feather bed and spent the night on it.

We carried buckets of water from the tap by the gate, which came from a well. We shared this with out next door farmer neighbour, Basil Hobby. In later years Joy married his brother Trevor, at the lovely little church along the lane.

We found an altar frontal in a chest in the vestry; it was embroidered in gold leaf thread. My husband and I restored it , and it was put back on the altar.

The Price's from Builth helped us to decorate the church, white washing walls, painting floor tiles, their daughter married there later. It is a peaceful church, steeped in prayer, and faithful Albert Price, went to church every Sunday.

Eventually we put water in the house, a toilet and a shower, but retained old beams and the character.

Bryntegan is mentioned in Kilvert's Diary, we owned it from 1959 until 1997, when sadly Barrie, developed Alzheimer's disease, and it was sold.

I must go back to John. He married a girl, Carol, he met in the office at the Coop. They started out in rooms, as we did. They now own their own house, both of them worked to get it, also giving Barrie and me two lovely grandchildren! Why must they grow up? There has been lots of heartache for all of us, but John and Carol have fought their own battles as we did. It's a different world today.

Muriel Arnall

PHOTOGRAPHS

Muriel Arnall with her teddy bear.
At Rose Cottage, Bromsgrove

Murial and Jack Arnall in the garden at Rednal.

Muriel Arnall with a friend

Muriel and Barry with their children

Haymaking

Joy & Trevor with Ceasar

An early photograph of Bryntegan

The heavy snow of 1963

Bringing the hay home!

George Palmer as a young man at Rednal

George & Ellen Palmer

Grandad Arnall

Grandma May Arnall

Barrington John Arnall

Haymaking

Printed in Great Britain
by Amazon